The Encyclopedia of
Beading
Techniques

The Encyclopedia of
Beading
Techniques

A step-by-step visual guide, with an
inspirational gallery of finished works

Sara Withers and
Stephanie Burnham

SEARCH PRESS

A QUARTO BOOK

Published in 2005 by Search Press Ltd
Wellwood
North Farm Road
Tunbridge Wells
Kent TN2 3DR
United Kingdom

Reprinted 2006 (three times), 2007 (twice), 2008 (twice), 2009 (twice), 2010

A catalogue record for this book is available from the
British Library.

Conceived, designed, and produced by
Quarto Publishing Plc
The Old Brewery
6 Blundell Street
London
N7 9BH

QUAR.EBD

Project Editor: Liz Pasfield
Art Editor: Claire van Rhyn
Assistant Art Director: Penny Cobb
Designer: Jill Mumford
Copy Editor: Claire Waite Brown
Photographers: Colin Bowling and Paul Forrester
Picture Research: Claudia Tate
Indexer: Pamela Ellis

Art Director: Moira Clinch
Publisher: Paul Carslake

Manufactured by Universal Graphics, Singapore
Printed in China by Toppan Leefung Printing Limited

CONTENTS

INTRODUCTION

Beads have played an important part in the lives of various peoples since prehistory, and are invaluable to archaeologists and historians looking to understand human societies since the very earliest of times. Beads were used to show status, as a form of portable wealth and as a means of trading. They have been formed into wearable works of art for many centuries – just think of the complexity of Egyptian beadwork that can date back to around 2500 BC. There are many excellent books that cover the complexity of the history of beads and outline the huge range of beads produced around the world. This book, on the other hand, illustrates the materials, tools and techniques that you can use to create your own works of art using the many varieties of bead available to today's bead worker.

Getting started

Bead workers often specialize in particular techniques: there are those who make jewellery and other objects using strung or wired beads; embroiderers who incorporate beads into their designs; and those who weave together mainly small beads, or small beads with featured individual beads. The book has therefore been organized into sections that relate to different uses of beads. We hope that you will enjoy and be inspired by the techniques covered. These practical chapters are complemented by an expansive Gallery section, featuring the work of some of the most prestigious designers in the field of beadwork, illustrating the creative spirit.

Supplies of beads, tools, findings, wires and threads are now more easily available than ever since the established bead shops and mail-order services are complemented by online bead suppliers. It is fascinating to consider the multi-ethnicity of the beads that you will be using. Many other countries also have bead societies that make useful sources of information about suppliers, bead history and other bead-related issues.

Evolving

Remember that this book should serve as a starting point for your exploration of working with beads. The techniques that are discussed can be adapted to achieve many different results and used to create decorative items as well as jewellery. The featured designers in the Gallery have demonstrated very impressively how amazing the results can be when individual creativity is added to the basic beading techniques. So now it is your turn to learn and enjoy the versatility of working with beads.

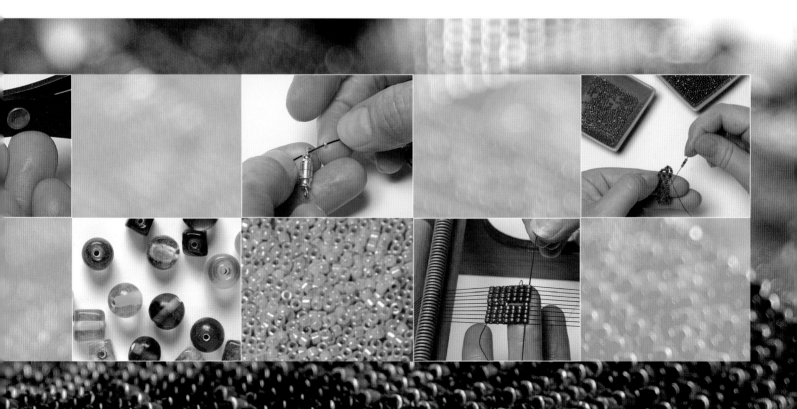

CTION 1
ls and Materials

king with beads, it is possible to achieve very impressive
out needing to invest in a huge range of tools and
You can start with a small selection and build up your
s you develop your skills. Look through the techniques
vered in this book and you will quickly discover the
adwork that appeal to you, and which items of
you will need to start practising.

buy beads, threads, wires, tools and findings from
ead suppliers, either from their shops, on the internet
gue mail order. You will also find supplies in craft and
s, and it is worth looking for tools in regular hardware
r working environment is also worth considering when
Good lighting and seating are of the utmost importance
either your eyes nor back are strained during long
working with beads.

Tools

Not all of the tools used for beadwork need to be sourced from specialist suppliers. Your local hardware shop will no doubt stock some of them. However, while it is possible to find very reasonably priced tools, remember that very cheap ones can be difficult to use.

1 Round-nosed pliers
2 Flat-, snipe-, or
   chain-nosed pliers
3 Blunt-nosed pliers
4 Crimping pliers
5 Split-ring pliers
6 Wire cutters
7 Cup bur

8 Files
9 Hammer and block
10 Jig
11 Loom
12 Needles
13 Tweezers
14 Reamer

ROUND-NOSED PLIERS

If you are working with wire, you will need round-nosed pliers **(1)**. Aim to choose a good pair with neat, short "noses", which will allow you to make small, neat loops and maintain good control of the work.

FLAT-, SNIPE- OR CHAIN-NOSED PLIERS

These terms refer to pliers that taper towards a flat end **(2)**. They can be used when working with wire and when attaching findings, such as French crimps or calottes. You will need a neat

pair, ensuring that the insides of the "noses" are smooth. Whether you choose sprung or unsprung pliers is purely a personal choice.

BLUNT-NOSED PLIERS

Blunt-nosed pliers **(3)** do not taper towards their flat ends. They are especially useful when attaching leather crimps or spring ends to thongs.

CRIMPING PLIERS

These are not an essential piece of equipment, but if you are going to finish necklaces or bracelets with French crimps they can be a great help **(4)**.

SPLIT-RING PLIERS

Again, an optional extra. If any of the designs you work involve the use of split rings, these specialist pliers **(5)** will save your fingernails.

WIRE CUTTERS

Another important tool when working with wire, or for cutting the specialist beading threads. It is important to choose a pair of wire cutters **(6)** with small, neat, pointed ends that will go in closely to the work. If you are using memory wire, you will also need either very heavy-duty cutters or special memory wire cutters.

CUP BUR

A cup bur **(7)** is designed to smooth the ends of wires. If you are going to make your own earwires, it is an excellent piece of equipment.

A wooden loom will give you the flexibility you need when creating loomed pieces.

Although seen as a specialist item, many beaders find that a necklace planning board is a useful part of the design process.

FILES

Files (8) can be used to smooth the cut ends of wire.

HAMMER AND BLOCK

Although heading into the arena of metalwork, these tools can be well worth exploring for flattening wire (9). Try experimenting with hammers you already have around the house, and look at the effects of hammering onto textured surfaces.

JIG

Jigs (10) for use with wire have been developed in recent years, and are only available from specialist suppliers.

LOOM

Looms (11) are available in several forms, from very inexpensive start-up kits to smart wooden ones. Generally speaking the less expensive metal or plastic versions are less easy to use, so again if you enjoy working on a loom, it is well worth buying a good one. For simple pieces of weaving it would also be possible to experiment by making a frame with nails at either end to wind your warp threads around, although this will not provide any flexibility.

NEEDLES

If you plan to do any beadweaving, knotting or loomwork, you will need a selection of needles (12). In some instances, such as when threading up a loom or making knots between beads, you will need strong, blunt-ended needles. For beadweaving there are specialist fine beading needles to work into very small beads. Specialist needles that are split by an "eye" that runs right down the centre are ideal for loomwork.

TWEEZERS

Available from specialist suppliers, tweezers (13) designed to be used for beading techniques have curved, pointed ends. They can be used to undo mistakes in knotting or to move knots. You should be careful not to damage their ends.

REAMER

Reamers (14) are designed to clear and smooth the centres of rough beads to ensure the least amount of wear on the threads.

NECKLACE PLANNING BOARD

Many people consider a necklace planning board (pictured above) useful in the design stage of necklaces. It is certainly a good tool to stop beads rolling away, but again it is a personal choice as to whether you use one or not.

Threads

There are a wide variety of threads available from the same sources as beadwork tools and findings. You can also explore fabric or embroidery shops to find some new ideas for yourself. You will need to consider the weight of your beads and the size of their holes when choosing threads – always choose the strongest thread possible, but remain aware that you want movement and flexibility in your designs.

Polyester threads and specialist beading wires are all extremely strong. You will find guidance as to which threads to choose by looking at the individual techniques in this book. As always, when you have mastered the techniques you can adapt your own designs by using different materials.

1 Beading wire
2 Tiger tail
3 Polyester thread
4 Nymo™ thread
5 Silk threads
6 Linen thread
7 Cotton thongs

8 Leather thongs
9 Hemp thread
10 Fine, clear elastic
11 Beeswax
12 Thread conditioner
13 Precoiled memory wire

BEADING WIRE AND TIGER TAIL

Beading wire (1) and tiger tail (2) are multistrands of very fine steel cables that are coated with plastic or nylon. They are both quick and easy to use without needles, and available in a variety of gauges. Some of the beading wires can be knotted but, in common with tiger tail, they are easy to finish with French crimps. Tiger tail is less expensive and is an excellent multipurpose thread, but can kink while being used and shear when in use.

SYNTHETIC BEADING THREADS

Polyester thread (3) makes a strong beading thread that is usually worked with needles. You will need to allow extra length for this, or in case the ends fray. This synthetic thread is available in different thicknesses, and the thicker thread is often waxed to aid threading.

Nymo™ (4) is a very fine synthetic thread used in beadwork.

NATURAL THREADS

Silk (5) and linen (6) threads are available in different thicknesses and colours, but are not as strong as the synthetic threads. Silk thread is usually supplied on cards with a useful integral needle.

Cotton (7) and leather thongs (8) are also available in different colours and thicknesses.

Hemp thread (9) is a natural thread most commonly used for knotting and braiding with featured beads.

ELASTIC

Fine, clear elastic (10) is available from bead suppliers, or thicker, round elastic can be bought as a sewing accessory.

THREAD CONDITIONER OR BEESWAX

Some of the beading threads you can buy are already waxed, but if not they can be conditioned with beeswax (11) or thread conditioner (12) to make them easy to work.

MEMORY WIRE

This is a very strong, precoiled wire (13) available in diameters that are suitable for chokers, bracelets or rings. It needs to be cut with great care using heavy-duty tools. It is included in the threading section because it can't be used with wiring techniques and is an alternative material on which to thread beads.

METAL WIRES

These are supplied by bead shops and suppliers, but precious metal wires and chains can also be bought from bullion suppliers.

Metal wires are supplied in a diverse range of finishes, sizes and shapes. Most bead stores will have supplies of copper (14), brass, silver (15) and gold wires, silver- and gold-plated wires (18) and colour-coated wires (16). It is important to differentiate between these and beading wires, which are nylon-coated and entirely different. In the world of beads, the latter tend to be referred to by their trade names to clarify this.

All the examples of wirework in this book, other than techniques that refer to earwires, have been made using silver-plated round wire. This is an excellent wire to practise with or to use in many designs. The 22 and 20 gauge (0.6 and 0.8mm diameter) wires in particular are good multipurpose wires. You will see from the chart (right) how the different gauges and diameters compare, and you may have to use either

measurement when purchasing wires. The finer gauge wires may prove to be too fragile for much more than decoration. The larger diameter wires are dramatic, but are difficult to work.

Using coloured wires is a great way to extend your design potential, but they can mark while you work with them, and the colour can wear with very heavy use.

When working with precious metal wires, look for the "half-hard" variety, which will be easier to use than a very soft wire that can "drift" rather than working precisely.

Always protect your eyes when cutting the ends of metal wire. Also be sure to use generous lengths of wire so that you don't hurt your hands by wrestling with short ends. Small pieces of precious metal wires can be kept to melt down.

METAL CHAINS

Chains (17) are available in both precious and plated metals. When choosing them, you will need to match the size of the links to the gauge of the wire you will be using with them. Also think about your budget, since chains can be expensive.

WIRE GAUGE AND DIAMETER	
Gauge	Approx. diameter (mm)
• 26	0.4mm
• 24	0.5mm
• 22	0.6mm
• 20	0.8mm
• 18	1.0mm
• 16	1.3mm
• 14	1.6mm

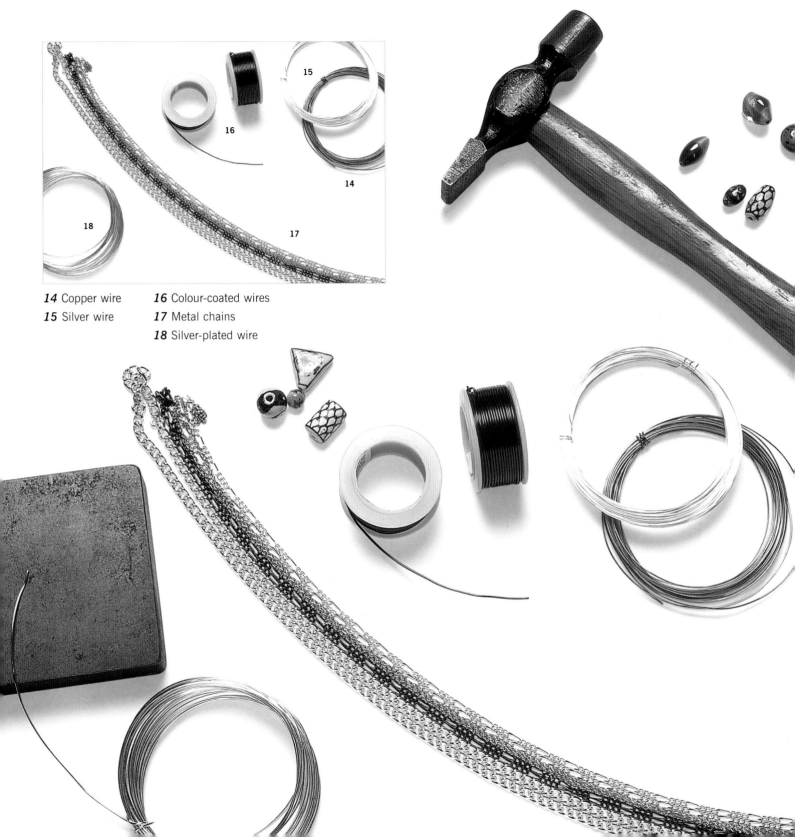

14 Copper wire
15 Silver wire
16 Colour-coated wires
17 Metal chains
18 Silver-plated wire

Beads

It only takes a trip to a local bead shop or a surf on the internet to discover just how many different shapes, sizes, colours and textures of beads there are available, and when you first start to explore the possibilities, the process can seem a little daunting. When purchasing beads, "you get what you pay for", so always try to buy the best you can afford. Stay well away from cheap beads because you will end up discarding more broken or misshapen beads than finding good ones you can use. Cheaper beads also tend to have sharp, uneven edges that may well cause the beading thread to break.

HISTORICALLY SPEAKING

Ever since historians and archaeologists started to study the origins and progress of mankind, beads have been of huge importance. People throughout time have adorned themselves with any material they could work with, such as shells or bones. Beads have also been essential trading properties throughout history.

    The descriptions of the beads listed here are intended only as a brief insight. If you become passionate about the beads themselves, there are excellent books devoted to their history, and societies established relevant to their study.

GLASS BEADS

Glass beads possibly come in the greatest variety of shapes, sizes and nationalities. They vary from collectable beads, such as millefiores, through to the tiny delicas that are associated with beadwork (see Seed Beads, page 20). The glass beads that are used in bead jewellery making have an infinite scope for use, from displaying one splendid bead as a pendant, to complex multistrand necklaces. Most glass beads are much stronger than you might suspect, but it is a good idea to try to ascertain their strength before embarking on really complex work. Some glass beads can also be a bit rough on the inside or at the edges of the hole, so try to use as strong a thread as possible with them – if they are very rough, you can use a bead reamer to smooth in and around the holes.

◄ Dichroic beads

Several companies are making glass for the growing number of glass artists producing beads.

► Czech Republic beads

The largest manufacturer of glass beads in the mid-nineteenth century was the former Czechoslovakia. These are faceted matt glass beads, some with a special *Aurora Borealis* (a.b.) finish (**1**). Contemporary pressed glass beads designed for Muslim pilgrims (**2**).

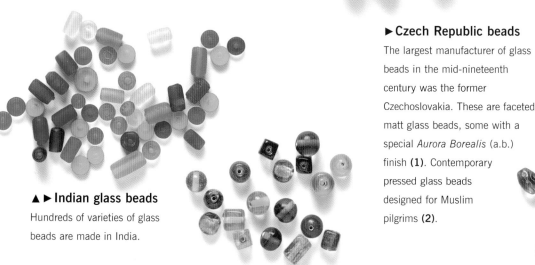

▲ ► Indian glass beads

Hundreds of varieties of glass beads are made in India.

◄Austrian crystal glass

Beads from the famous Swarovski company that has been in production for many years.

◄Glass-blown beads

These beads are hand blown by craftsmen from hollow tubes of glass, then surface decorated.

▲Venetian glass foil beads

An ancient technique still in use today.

▲Venetian millefiore beads

Mainly made during the nineteenth century, although some date from much earlier.

▼American furnace beads

Drawn hollow cane beads made by glass artists in the U.S.

▲Ghanaian powder glass beads

These beads are made mainly from crushed soft drinks bottles, then layered, coloured and refired.

PLASTIC BEADS

There is a multitude of plastic beads, from cheap, brightly coloured beads that are mostly associated with children, to very collectable plastics such as Bakelite. Between these come acrylics and many designer-made polymer clay beads. Recent years have seen a large-scale production of metallized plastic/plastic beads with a metal-like coating.

▶Metallized plastic

European plastic beads covered in a very durable plastic coating in different finishes.

▲Resin from Indonesia

A comparatively new material for bead making, and used in many shapes and colours.

▼Naive plastic

Cheap and cheerful plastic beads.

▼Children's beads

Inexpensive beads often used for, or by, children.

▲Polymer clay

Generally individually made by "polymer artists", these beads are also mass produced in the Far East.

SEED BEADS

These round beads, also known as rocaille, are produced in Japan, Czechoslovakia, India, France and China, and are available in a wide variety of sizes, including 6, 8, 11 and 15 (mm), and in many different finishes. All these beads work well for most of the beadweaving techniques, including freeform work, since they are round, polished beads that blend and mould together well.

Japanese seed beads in sizes 8, 11 and 15.

▼ Triangle beads

Triangle beads are generally available in sizes 5, 8 and 10mm, in a very wide range of colours and finishes. They give great added shape and texture to a design. Although the beads are triangular in shape, the hole through the centre of the bead is sometimes round. This does not affect the bead in any way, and interestingly enough, triangle beads sit very well next to each other when working such stitches as peyote and herringbone, quite like the scales of an animal.

▼ Bugle beads

These long, cylindrical tubes are available in several sizes including 4 and 6mm. Most seed beads are "tumbled" while in the factory, but bugle beads generally are not, which can mean the ends are very sharp, often resulting in broken thread. It is well worth discarding these, and buying the best quality available. The Japanese bugles tend to be very smooth-edged, but you still need to keep an eye out for sub-standard beads.

▲ Cube beads

The most commonly used and often easiest size to locate are 4mm cubes. Generally they have round holes through the centre and are available in a large range of colours and finishes. They are popular with designers because the beads have straight edges which give designs added strength and stability.

▲ Japanese cylinder beads

These are small cylinder beads with an extra large hole. They are among the most regular, uniform beads you will find in the world today. Due to the way these beads sit together, they are wonderful for creating pictorial or patterned beadwork. These beads are unmistakable due to their extreme high quality.

SELECTING BEAD COLOURS AND SIZES

It may be tempting to choose subtle, toning shades of beads, because they look great in their tubes, but be aware that you are looking at a "block" of colour within the tube, which intensifies the hue. When the beads are applied singly, the colours diffuse and subtle colours can look washed out. Remember that "loud" colours will calm down dramatically when applied one at a time, so try to be bold when choosing colours. If it's possible, tip one or two beads into your hand to view the true colour.

HOW MANY BEADS?

Even if a pattern or book project states how many grams of each bead are required, always buy more than you need. Beads are made and dyed in batches, so if you have to buy more beads to finish a piece, you may well find that the new beads vary in colour to those in the rest of the project. Also, beading is at the height of its popularity, and because there is such a demand for beads worldwide, it might be quite some time before your bead stockist has more supplies in, or – in rare instances – the colour may be discontinued.

METAL BEADS

Different societies have created beads from a range of metals from the earliest ages of metalworking, either from highly prized metals, such as gold and silver, or base metals, such as copper, brass and aluminium. Tin cooking pots are recycled into beads in Kenya, while gold and silver are worked into exquisite designs in Bali and other Far Eastern countries. In Thailand, Cambodian refugees have developed a way of making a pitch base for beads that are then covered in silver or gold. European countries make ranges of plated metal beads that are very distinctive.

► Indian brass

Brass beads are produced in many different shapes and sizes, and in many parts of the world. The examples shown here are Indian.

▲ ► Greek metal

Made from non-precious metals, these beads are produced in a wide range of sizes and finishes.

◄ Balinese silver

Silver beads are made in many parts of the world, but Balinese craftspeople specialize in making a huge range of very fine beads.

◄ Welsh metal

Another example of the universality of bead manufacturing, these beads are designed and made by a small company in Wales.

◄ ▼ Cambodian/Thai silver

These beads are made in Thailand using a traditional Cambodian technique that involves covering a pitch "body" with silver or gold.

► Indian aluminium

These beads, which are generally an aspect of recycling, are made using very basic techniques by Indian bead makers, in many different designs.

ORGANIC MATERIALS

The list of organic materials used to make beads, and the designs created from them, is extensive. Beads made from pearls, wood, shell, bone, different varieties of drilled and shaped nuts and seeds, to name a just few, are the oldest beads known to mankind.

◀ German wooden beads

These beads are produced by a toy manufacturer.

◀ Kakui nuts

Just one example of the wide range of seeds and nuts that are drilled, sometimes colored or polished, and used as beads.

▼ Amber

Fossilized tree resin many millions of years old is a coveted material for bead making.

▶ Shell

Since the birth of civilization, all sorts of shells, from the sea or land, have been drilled and threaded.

▼ Horn

Usually from water buffalo or cattle, this material can be shaped, stained or polished and is often used to emulate another material, such as amber.

▲ Wooden beads

Different woods are used all over the world to make beads. The speckled ones here are made from palm wood. Other woods are polished, stained, carved and painted. Another notable wood is sandalwood, prized for its smell, but now protected.

▲ Freshwater pearls

These pearls are produced by inserting grit into the shell of molluscs to encourage them to produce nacre to cover the grit, forming the small, bumpy pearls.

▶ Bone

Bone is used in similar ways to horn, being coloured and carved into different shapes and designs. Often a surface colour is applied then carved through, as shown here.

▶ Limestone
Some stones have achieved a specific status, such as semi-precious or precious, but more common stones, such as limestone, also make beautiful beads.

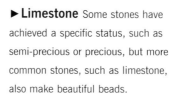

CERAMIC BEADS

Ceramic beads are produced in most areas of the world, again in a huge variety of finishes and designs. Egyptian faience beads were one of the forerunners of bead production. Now we have beautiful ceramic beads from Peru, Kenya and Greece, among other places.

▶ Indian ceramic

These beads were made in small workshops in Rajasthan. They are glazed in striking colours, but are rather delicate.

▲ Kenyan ceramic

The beads shown are made by hand in a workshop in Nairobi that was established to help single mothers in the city.

▼ Greek ceramic

A huge range of different designs and shapes of beads are made as a result of the traditional use of "worry" beads by Greek men. The beads shown here have a transfer design on them.

▼ Peruvian ceramic

These delicate beads from Peru were originally made by traditional methods in one village. They became immensely popular in the 1980s and 1990s and the production was vastly increased and modernized, causing problems when the beads ceased to be so desirable.

SEMI-PRECIOUS BEADS

This heading encompasses an enormous list of materials and shapes, produced in all corners of the world. Just stop to think about turquoise, lapis lazuli, carnelian and malachite. Not only have they been used for adornment throughout the history of mankind, they have also formed one of the basic elements of trading.

▼ Turquoise beads

Turquoise was first mined in the Sinai desert more than 6,000 years ago. It is still produced in many different areas, the largest quantities in the south west of America.

▼ Lapis lazuli

This semi-precious stone is lazurite mixed with calcite and pyrite. The former gives the white flecks in the stones, and the latter the "gold" flecks. It is mined and prized all over the world.

▶ Hematite

Specular hematite is the semi-precious form of the mineral, which is generally used in bead making.

▶ Malachite

Malachite is an altered form of copper, which is popular as a semi-precious stone because of the beautiful banding in the colour. Malachite beads tend to be associated with Africa and are commonly used in jewellery from Zambia and Zimbabwe.

▶ Dalmatian jasper

These stones are forms of non-crystalline quartz. There are many different types of jasper, such as picture jasper, red jasper or the Dalmatian jasper shown here.

Findings

Findings can be purchased from bead or craft shops, internet sites or by mail order from bead suppliers. This book illustrates examples of the main types of findings used, but remember that there is an enormous variety available, and findings can often be adapted for other uses. Most findings will be available in plated or pure metals, in silver or gold colours; however, using sterling silver or gold for earwires is advisable. Also remember – if you choose magnetic clasps – the issue of safety for people who have a pacemaker.

Bead caps

These findings can be threaded on either side of beads for decoration or protection.

French crimps

You can use French crimps to attach fasteners to beading wire and threads, or to build up designs.

Cones and end caps

Cones and end caps can be used to finish multistrands in earrings, necklaces or bracelets.

End bars

Use end bars to finish the end of a multirow necklace or bracelet.

Leather crimps and spring ends

Leather crimps (1) and spring ends (2) are used to attach fasteners to leather or cotton thongs.

Calottes and clamshell calottes

These can be used to attach a fastener to a thread or wire necklace or bracelet.

Spacer bars

These findings space the strands on a multirow necklace or bracelet.

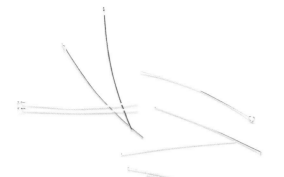

Eyepins and headpins

Eyepins and headpins support the beads in a drop earring.

Ear posts

The ear post is used as a mount for stones or to be glued to cabochons.

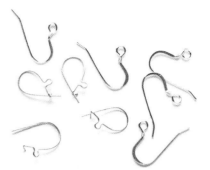

Earwires and ear studs

These both go into the ear to suspend drops.

Multirow fasteners

Fasteners designed specifically for use with a multirow necklace or bracelet.

Scrolls or butterflies

These fit on the back of pierced-ear findings to hold them in the ear.

Screw or clip ear findings

Use these findings for earrings for non-pierced ears.

Fasteners

Screw **(1)**, trigger **(2)**, T-bar **(3)**, hook and eye **(4)**, magnetic **(5)** – any of these fasteners can be chosen to fasten necklaces or bracelets.

Jump rings

Circles of metal used for linking or with hooks as a fastener.

Split rings

Double circles of metal are more secure for the same uses as jump rings.

SECTION 2
Techniques

The aim of this book is to separate and highlight the various techniques that can be combined to produce beautiful results with beads. Each technique can be used with different types of beads, often to produce surprisingly different results. The techniques have generally been linked with jewellery-making, but you can also experiment with making decorative or household items.

BEAD EMBROIDERY

Beads can be used on many different media. They don't even have to be sewn on: they can also be pinned, as on Victorian pincushions, or glued. As beads have moved to the forefront of interior design, fashion and textiles, and they become more and more popular with designers and general crafters, the choice and availability of beads has increased greatly.

Bead embroidery on fabric

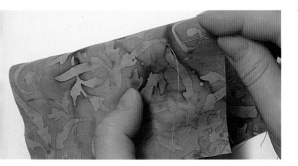

Choose a selection of coloured beads based around the colours in the fabric, making sure there is just enough tonal difference for the beads to stand out.

Beads can be sewn onto any fabric you can get a needle through, and they look great on bags, hats, clothes, shoes and belts, to name but a few. The sample here has been worked on an interesting piece of fabric with a "dyed" effect. Both bugle and seed beads have been applied to enhance the shapes and colours within the fabric.

1 Thread a short beading needle with 1m (1 yard) of thread and tie a knot at the other end. Bring the needle out through the front of the fabric where you wish to position the first bead.

2 Thread on the first bead, then take the needle down through the fabric, slightly farther along from where the thread came up. Leaving a slight gap between the entrance and exit of the thread allows space for the bead to sit nicely. Continue to embellish with beads in the same way until you are happy with the finished look. If you wish to create areas of beadwork, you need to finish the working thread off and start a new thread where you wish the next area of embellishment to be placed.

You can add several beads at one time if you wish.

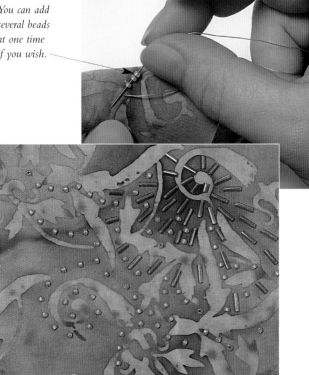

TOOLS AND MATERIALS
- Short beading needle
- Beading thread
- Cotton sewing thread
- Bugle and seed beads

Embellished papers are perfect for bead embroidery.

Bead embroidery on paper

Paper crafts are enjoying a huge revival, helped largely by the wealth of beautiful papers currently being produced. Among them are papers that have already been embellished with machine embroidery. These are perfect for bead embellishment because the holes to thread the needle through have already been made by the sewing machine. As with bead embroidery on fabric, you can use seed and bugle beads.

1 Gather together some beads to work with, a beading needle and some beading thread or cotton sewing thread, in a colour that tones well with the paper.

This selvage gives you enough spare paper to cover a book or notepad.

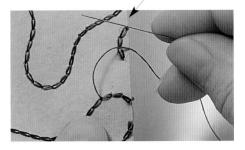

2 Thread a beading needle with 1m (1 yard) of thread and tie a knot at the other end. Leaving a selvage about 2cm (¾ inch) in from the outside edge of the paper, bring the needle up through the back of the paper to the front, using one of the machined holes.

TOOLS AND MATERIALS

- Beading or cotton sewing thread
- Beading needle

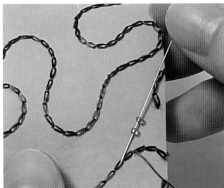

3 Look carefully at the gap between the hole the thread is coming out of and the next machined hole along to decide how many beads can fit into that space: in this instance, using size 11 seed beads, there is room for two beads to be threaded on. Thread on the beads and take the needle down through the next hole along.

5 Continue adding beads in the same way. When you get to the end of a row or aspect of the pattern – remembering to leave another 2cm (¾ inch) selvage – you can turn the paper around and stitch back to the start, adding on beads to fill the gaps left by the first row of embroidery. There is also nothing to stop you sewing through the paper itself to create extra embellishment.

Any gaps in the beading can be filled in on the return journey.

4 Bring the needle up through the next hole along, ready to add on the next beads. This leaves a gap that can either be filled on the return journey, perhaps with a contrasting bead, or left as it is to let some of the initial machine stitching show through.

Use bugle beads to form a flower pattern.

Beaded fringing

Decorative fringing can enhance household items, such as cushions, curtains and throws, and create stunning effects when applied to clothing and fashion accessories.

You can choose to apply any length of fringe, depending on the look required. In this example a beaded fringe has been added to a scarf.

A mixture of crystal, seed and bugle beads work well for fringing.

1 When choosing beads, make sure they tone with the colours within the item you are going to embellish. Using varying sizes of beads can be effective. For this technique some crystal beads are used alongside bugle and seed beads. Beading thread or cotton sewing thread can be used. Remember to choose a thread colour that matches the main colour in the fabric, since you will be able to see it, ever so slightly.

2 Lay the fabric out flat on the working surface, with the edge you wish to fringe closest to you. The edge needs to be hemmed, so if you are not using a ready-made item, add a roughly 5cm (2 inch) hem. Using a ruler, place pins in the positions for each fringe: for this example the pins have been placed 1cm (⅜ inch) apart.

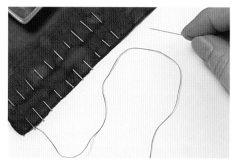

3 Thread a long beading needle with about 2m (2 yards) of beading thread. Take the needle down through the edge of the fabric and secure the thread with a double knot.

TOOLS AND MATERIALS
- Beading or cotton sewing thread
- Ruler
- Pins
- Long beading needle
- Crystal, bugle and seed beads

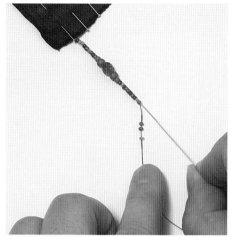

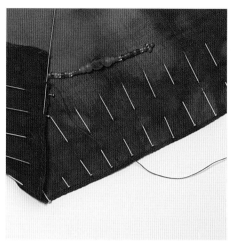

4 Practise threading on beads in a range of patterns until you are happy with the overall look. You may need to do this several times. The inclusion of crystal beads here gives added weight to the fringe, making it drape nicely.

5 To return, skip the last three beads and thread the needle up through the remaining beads until you reach the fabric once again. As you do this, be aware of "the dangle factor": too loose and the beading thread will show between the fabric and the fringe, too tight and the beaded fringe will appear buckled and will not hang well.

6 Take the needle back into the hem of the fabric. Working on the wrong side of the fabric, use tiny running stitches along the hem to take you to the next pin position.

7 Continue adding fringes in the same way. You can repeat the same beading pattern each time, or make changes to each fringe. You could add more beads as you work each fringe to create a point in the centre; just count the number of pins so you know where the centre fringe should be.

8 To complete the look, sew back along the very edge of the fabric – using the original seam machine stitching as a guide when working on a ready-made item – adding a size 8, a size 6 and a size 8 seed bead between each fringe drop. This finishes the fringe off perfectly.

THREADING

Potential bead jewellery-makers usually ask the same three questions. How are fasteners attached? What are the best threads to use? Are knots essential? These questions are answered in this section on threading and design, and the examples used illustrate some of the wide range of results that can be achieved using basic techniques. It is also important to consider, as this section does, ways of adapting the techniques into different designs for each maker's own use.

Working with thongs

Greek ceramic beads and bone spacers on a leather thong, with a ceramic sliding bead.

A few special beads on a thong make a simple piece of beaded jewellery that is likely to be the first item a novice maker chooses. These can be finished in different ways, with beads, knots or fasteners and findings.

SLIDING BEADS

The most simple way to fasten a necklace, bracelet or anklet.

1 Cut a piece of thong that is long enough to go over your head. Add your chosen beads, knotting beside them if you wish. Thread both ends of the leather into another bead that is strong and fits tightly. This is the sliding bead.

2 Knot each end of the leather, so that the sliding bead cannot slip off. The sliding bead can be moved up or down to adjust the length of the necklace when worn.

BEADING TIP

Allow extra length for knots beside the beads.

SLIDING KNOTS

Another simple way to finish a basic necklace.

1 Cut a piece of thong that is long enough to go over your head and thread on your beads. Place the ends of the thong so that they overlap and sit across from each other.

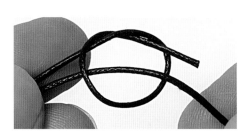

2 Pass the left-hand end over and back under the right-hand thong next to it. Now pass the left end back over itself, and through, to form a knot.

3 Move the right-hand end over the left-hand thong, back over itself and through, facing away from the first knot. Tighten both knots, leaving a short end outside them so that they won't unravel. These sliding knots can be moved up or down to adjust the length of the necklace when worn.

Indian glass beads on a leather thong with sliding knots.

SPRING ENDS

These are findings suitable for use with thongs or very thick threads.

A broader flat nose on the pliers will be helpful.

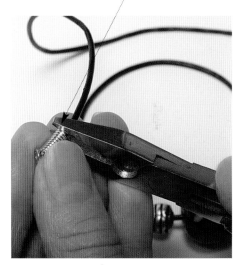

1 Cut a piece of thong to your chosen length, remembering that the fastener will add a little to this length. Thread on the beads, putting knots beside them if preferred. Put a spring end on one end of the thong and use blunt-nosed pliers to squeeze the last row of springs into the thong. Check that it is tight enough to grip into the thong without damaging it. Repeat with the second spring end on the other end of the thong.

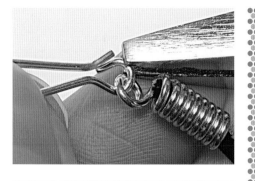

2 Add a hook to one spring end by using the pliers to open its loop sideways. Attach the opened loop to the spring end and close again with the pliers.

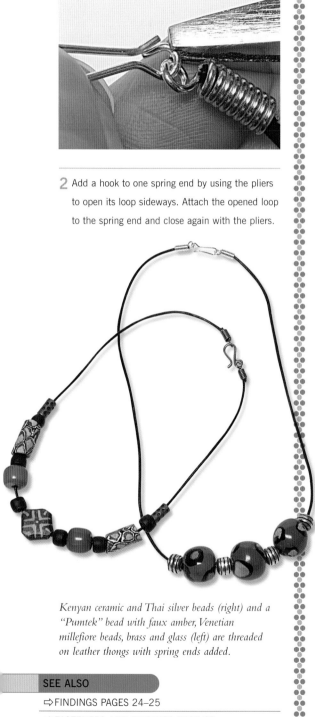

Kenyan ceramic and Thai silver beads (right) and a "Pumtek" bead with faux amber, Venetian millefiore beads, brass and glass (left) are threaded on leather thongs with spring ends added.

SEE ALSO

⇨FINDINGS PAGES 24–25

⇨FASTENERS AND FINDINGS PAGE 69

LEATHER CRIMPS

Another finding designed for use with thongs or thick threads.

1 Cut the leather thong to fit and thread on the beads. Place one end of the thong into a leather crimp. Use blunt-nosed pliers to fold one side of the crimp around the leather. Repeat with the other side of the crimp, squeezing until the leather is held firmly.

TOOLS AND MATERIALS

- Leather thong
- Two leather crimps
- Blunt-nosed pliers
- Hook, either a ready-made hook or one you have made

Your fasteners will be attached to the loops at the top of the crimps.

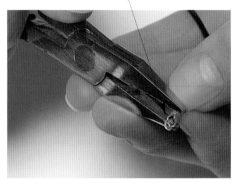

2 Attach the other leather crimp to the other end of the thong in the same way. Add a hook to one leather crimp (see Spring Ends page 33) or add a screw fastener (see Findings page 24–25) to both ends.

Dichroic glass and Thai silver beads on a leather thong with leather crimps and a hook.

Indian glass and Greek metal bead necklace with French crimps and fastener.

Finishing beading wire or thread

There is now a wide selection of threads available for bead jewellery-making, and a huge selection of findings that go with them. The findings and threads are discussed individually on pages 14–17 and 24–25. The techniques that are used to combine them are explained here.

Remember that most of these techniques can be adapted for use with different materials. Most of the techniques in this section are used with beading wires, but they can also apply to strong synthetic threads. Once the basics have been mastered, each maker will extend their own skills.

FRENCH CRIMPING

When working with the new specialist threading materials, such as tiger tail and other similar beading wires, you will need to learn how to crimp the ends of your work to attach a fastener.

1 Cut a length of beading wire, allowing 3–4cm (1 ¼–1 ½ inches) extra at each end to attach the fastener, using wire cutters or heavy-duty scissors – good scissors will be spoiled by the wire. Thread on your beads. Thread a French crimp on one end of the wire, then thread the wire through the fastener.

2 Thread the beading wire back through the French crimp, leaving a loop that allows movement but looks neat.

Use two French crimps if you have heavy beads.

3 Now flatten the French crimp with crimping pliers or blunt-nosed pliers. Slide the beads up to meet the crimp, passing them over the loose end of the thread if possible; if not, cut the loose end very close to the crimp then slide back the beads. Add another French crimp to the other end of the wire and attach the other end of the fastener as before, allowing for some movement but without the thread showing too much.

TOOLS AND MATERIALS

- Wire cutters or very heavy-duty scissors
- Tape (optional)
- Crimping pliers or flat-nosed pliers

A barrel screw clasp and French crimps.

SEE ALSO

⇨FINDINGS PAGES 24–25

CALOTTES

The more flexible varieties of beading wires can be knotted at the ends, or between beads. These can be attached to the fastener using a calotte over the knot at the end of the strand. This is also a simple way to attach several strands of beads to a fastener.

A selection of calottes.

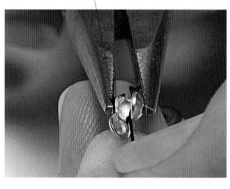

Look for the little groove in the calotte for the thread to sit in.

4 Depending on the type of fastener you are using, it can either be attached to the calotte by opening the loops on the fastener, or by gently opening the loop on the calotte, with pliers. Then clip off the ends of the beading wire.

1 Cut a length of beading wire, allowing 4–5cm (1 ½–2 inches) extra at each end to attach the fastener, using wire cutters or heavy-duty scissors. Thread on your beads. You may want to anchor one side of your work to the work surface with tape while you finish the other. Make an overhand knot in the other end of the wire.

2 Place the knot into a calotte and use flat-nosed pliers to gently squeeze it over the knot.

3 At the other end, make an overhand knot and put a blunt needle into it. Use the needle to slide the knot close, but not too close, to the beads. Squeeze another calotte over this knot.

Modern Venetian and glass beads on a necklace with calottes and an ornate fastener.

TOOLS AND MATERIALS

- Beading wire
- Wire cutters or very heavy-duty scissors
- Tape (optional)
- Two calottes
- Flat-nosed pliers
- Blunt needle
- Fastener

CALOTTES ON A MULTISTRAND PIECE

A larger calotte works well over knots or crimps to join several strands together in a necklace or bracelet.

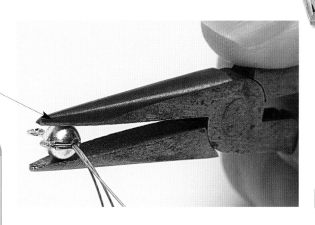

Multistrand Venetian bead necklace.

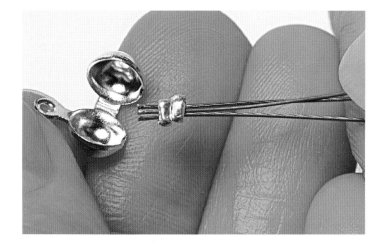

1 Use two French crimps to attach the strands of the necklace or bracelet together. Clip the ends of the threads, then put a calotte around them.

Squeeze firmly, but not so hard that the threads are damaged.

TOOLS AND MATERIALS

- Multistrand necklace or bracelet
- French crimps
- Wire cutters or heavy-duty scissors
- Tape (optional)
- Two calottes
- Flat-nosed pliers and crimping pliers
- Fastener

2 Squeeze the calotte together with flat-nosed pliers. Close it firmly enough to hold the strands in place without shearing them. Repeat on the other side and attach a fastener.

SEE ALSO

⇨ KNOTTING PAGES 46–57

⇨ FRENCH CRIMPING PAGE 35

⇨ FINDINGS PAGES 24–25

⇨ CRIMPING TO SPACE PAGE 41

CRIMPING ONTO AN END BAR OR MULTIROW CLASP

Other findings that can be used to create a multistrand effect are end bars or fasteners with several integral loops. These are available in a huge variety of different designs and can create many different looks.

End bars and a box fastener.

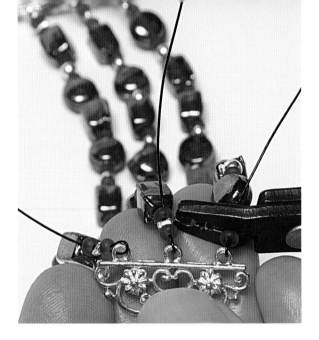

If you are using a multirow fastener, you will crimp straight onto the fastener.

1 You can thread your work first, then attach the end bars at both ends, but when working on a bracelet, it is easier to use French crimps to attach your threads to one end bar before beading. Then thread on your beads, working along the strands to balance them.

2 When the beads are in place, use more crimps to attach the bar at the other side. A fastener can now be attached if you have used end bars.

Fake pearls with a multirow clasp.

TOOLS AND MATERIALS
- Beading wire
- Wire cutters or heavy-duty scissors
- French crimps
- Two end bars or a multirow fastener
- Crimping pliers or flat-nosed pliers

FINISHING MULTISTRANDS INTO A CONE

Another approach when using many strands is to gather the ends together into a cone and make a feature of it. You could finish with knots or French crimps inside the cone. The latter would be quicker and probably more secure.

Ornate cones and beads.

Strands of small beads, birds, and hanging stars are connected by cones.

1 Make your strands of beads and check that they will hang together well by holding them up. Use French crimps to secure the ends, making small loops at the end of each thread.

2 Cut two new lengths of beading wire and make a simple loop at the end of each one. Gather the strands of beads, threading through the loops on each strand. Thread back into the new loops.

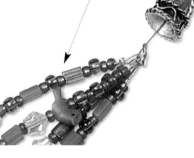

Check again to see how the strands hang together.

3 Now put a cone at each end of the necklace over all of the ends of the strands.

4 Thread more beads onto each of the single threads and crimp them onto a fastener.

TOOLS AND MATERIALS
- Strands of beads
- French crimps
- Flat-nosed pliers or crimping pliers
- Beading wire
- Wire cutters or heavy-duty scissors
- Two cones
- Fastener

SEE ALSO
⇨ FRENCH CRIMPING PAGE 35
⇨ BEADS AND WIRE PAGES 58–85
⇨ FINDINGS PAGES 24–25

Working with memory wire

Small glass bead bracelet on memory wire.

Although memory wire is a wire, it is essentially another threading material that can add diversity to necklace, bracelet or even ring designs. It is a very strong, precoiled wire that is supplied in three different diameters. It can be used in continuous lengths, or as separate strands connected by spacer bars.

FINISHING MEMORY WIRE WITH ROLLED ENDS

This is the easiest way to finish the ends of memory wire.

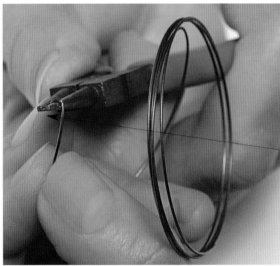

2 Roll one end of the wire with strong round-nosed pliers; again, don't use a delicate pair.

Take care when working with memory wire; the ends can be very sharp.

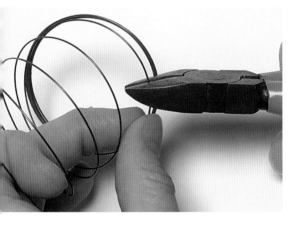

3 Thread on your beads, leaving about 6–7mm (¼ inch) at the end so that you can roll this end of the wire as well.

1 Cut the required amount of memory wire with strong wire cutters. Never use a delicate pair because they will be ruined by the wire.

TOOLS AND MATERIALS

- Very strong wire cutters
- Strong round-nosed pliers

BEADING TIP

It is also possible to buy special end caps that can be glued onto each end of the wire to finish it.

Variations in threading design

One of the main pleasures in making bead jewellery is taking time to experiment with different designs. Anything that doesn't work can easily be taken to pieces and reworked. Some different techniques in threading are shown in this section, remember to consider the techniques shown in Knotting on pages 46–57 as well.

When trying a different necklace design, it is a good idea to have a mirror within reach, so that the progress can be checked against a body rather than abstractly on a worktop. It is often surprisingly different.

Semi-precious beads on beading wire, with strands held together by a crimped loop.

CRIMPING VARIATIONS

French crimps can be used for purposes other than adding fasteners, and can in fact be integrated into your designs.

Crimping to space

Single strand or multistrand designs with spaces can be created with crimps.

Use French crimps on either side of the beads to create spaces between them. You may need to position a small bead beside the featured beads to stop the crimp going into the hole of the main bead.

You can either use a measure or assess your spaces by eye.

TOOLS AND MATERIALS
- Wire cutters or heavy-duty scissors
- French crimps
- Crimping pliers or flat-nosed pliers
- Fasteners

SEE ALSO
⇨ FRENCH CRIMPING PAGE 35
⇨ FINISHING BEADING WIRE OR THREAD PAGES 35–39
⇨ FINDINGS PAGES 24–25

Crimping to decorate

Crimps can be used to add sections to a design.

1 To create a fringed effect on a necklace or bracelet, join beaded sections together with a crimped loop at the top. Hold the beads in place with a crimp at the bottom of each strand.

The strength of the French crimps is important – however, they should not be too visible.

2 Use the loop at the top of the strands to thread them onto the work between other beads.

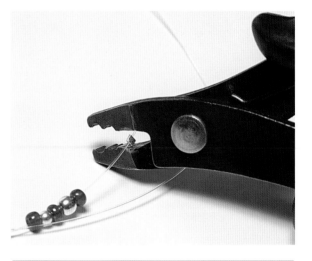

3 In this example short lengths of beading thread are attached to the main strand of beading wire with crimps. Then beads are crimped onto each of the short strands, which can be built up in a regular pattern or for a random effect.

Glass hearts on an "invisible" nylon thread.

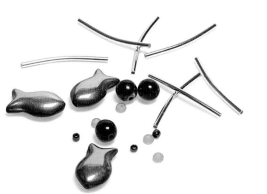

THREADING VARIATIONS

More examples of different ways in which beads can be threaded.

Y necklaces

This different shape for necklaces uses a single strand of wire or thread.

1 Cut a length of beading wire or thread, remembering to allow plenty of length for the drop. Start from the middle with a tiny, but strong, bead. Then bring the threads together through the central beads, so that the tiny bead will hold them in place.

Once these threads have been tightened, the beads will not be able to be repositioned.

2 Separate the threads when you have enough beads on the central drop. Choose some small beads for each strand first so that they will sit together well.

3 Continue to thread up each side of the necklace and attach to a fastener.

Glass fish and silver tube Y necklace.

TOOLS AND MATERIALS

- Wire cutters or heavy-duty scissors
- Crimping pliers or flat-nosed pliers
- Fasteners

Double-strand threading

This is a way to use two separate strands of beading wire or thread together to make the beads sit in a different direction. It is useful for bracelets or chokers.

Greek metal bead choker worked using the double-strand threading method.

2 Add a few more small beads to cover the threads between the beads, and thread into the next bead from either end. Continue in this way, crossing the threads inside the beads until you reach your desired length and you can finish off in the same way that you started. The same threading technique can be used with different approaches to the finishing, as in the leather choker.

1 Cut two lengths of beading wire or thread, two to three times the length of the bracelet that you intend to make, dependent on the length of the beads you are using. Crimp both threads to a fastener at one end. Separate the strands and add enough beads to cover them before you work into the first bead from either side.

Peruvian bead bracelet made with double strand threading.

Threading multistrands into featured beads

This is a technique that can be used in many different applications for necklaces, bracelets or even earrings. The strands of small beads work back into the featured beads to enhance their prominence, keeping the design neat and powerful.

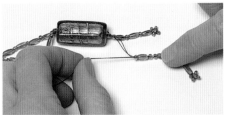

Use strong but fine threads – they have to go through some of the beads many times. This is a fine polyester thread that has been used double.

1 Use French crimps or knots to attach your thread to a fastener. Thread on the first strand of beads, spacing out feature beads between small beads. You can work with a continuous strand of beads with a featured central bead, in which case you will crimp or knot to the other side of your fastener at the other end. In this example a tassel effect is at the bottom of the design. Now attach your second thread.

2 Use a beading needle to thread the first section of small beads on the second strand as before, then thread back into the first featured bead. Continue in this way to complete each strand of beads, then repeat with the strands from the other side of the necklace.

4 Squeeze the crimp gently but firmly to hold the work in place. This technique will be repeated with the other strands from both sides of the design.

3 To finish as a tassel, pass your first threads through the main feature bead and add a small crimp and some more small beads to each strand to begin forming the tassel. At the end add a few tiny beads. Thread back up the main section of small beads, leaving the tiny beads to hold the strand in place. Work back through the crimp and pull the strand so that there are no gaps.

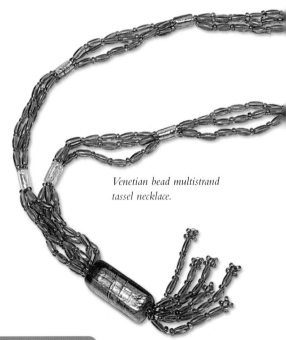

Venetian bead multistrand tassel necklace.

SEE ALSO

⇨ FINISHING BEADING WIRE OR THREAD PAGES 35–39

⇨ FRENCH CRIMPING PAGE 35

⇨ FINDINGS PAGES 24–25

KNOTTING

Knotting is one of the more traditional aspects of working with beads and there are various reasons for learning the techniques that are involved. When using the appropriate threads, knots provide a way to finish a necklace without needing much in the way of specialist tools or findings. The use of knots is also a very good way to make the most of a few special beads.

Traditionally knots were placed between beads to protect them from rubbing against each other and because in the past the threads couldn't be fully relied upon – if there were knots between the beads, only a couple of beads would be lost in the event of a breakage. This is less appropriate today, with the emergence of synthetic threads, but threads can still wear if there is roughness inside the beads.

Striped Indian beads on
a cotton thong.

Knotting to finish

> **BEADING TIP**
> The golden rule of knotting is to allow yourself plenty of thread.

Here are a few ways to finish necklaces or bracelets, with and without fasteners. Remember that with the use of all knots consideration must be given to the thickness of the threads in relation to the beads.

SINGLE KNOT TO FINISH

A simple reef knot at the back is sufficient for a long string of beads that will go over the head without a fastener.

> **BEADING TIP**
> Knots can also be used to repair old necklaces, which won't be long enough if they are rethreaded without the knots, unless spacer beads are used.

1 Thread the beads, allowing an extra 10–12cm (4–4 ¾ inches) of thread for the knot. Work the ends of the thread left over right.

2 Now work the ends right over left to form a reef knot. Tighten the knot so that it is firm, but not so tight against the beads that you make the thread stiff. Trim the ends of the thread.

KNOTTING AMONG FINISHING BEADS

This is a good way to finish a very long string of beads neatly. If they are finished this way, they could be worn double, because the thread ends are hidden within the beads. If you have a long string of heavy beads, you can make a flat back to your necklace using this technique. Remember that you will need to choose beads that will take a double thickness of thread.

2 Make a knot over the main thread by taking the short end of the thread over the main thread, back round over itself and through the loop.

3 Thread this end through the next bead and make another knot, using a blunt needle to guide this knot if necessary.

German wooden beads to wind around a wrist.

Finish with a small amount of glue or nail polish on the knots but be careful not to get any onto the beads.

1 Thread the beads, allowing plenty of thread at the end for the knots, around 10cm (4 inches) each side. Thread back into three beads on one side. If you are working in a centred design, you will need to put three extra beads on one side.

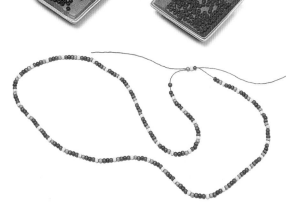

4 Now repeat on the other side of the string of beads and trim the ends of the thread. Thread the ends on down the string.

TOOLS AND MATERIALS

- Beading needle
- Blunt needle

SEE ALSO

⇨KNOTTING BETWEEN BEADS PAGES 52–54

KNOTTING ONTO A FASTENER

This is an easy way to attach a fastener without findings or specialist tools. This method can be used for beads that won't take two thicknesses of thread.

Use a needle with a large enough "eye".

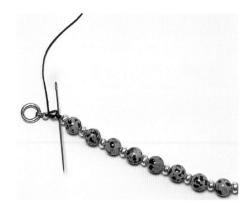

You can use a small amount of glue to finish but do not get any glue onto precious beads.

1 Thread the beads, allowing about 15cm (6 inches) of extra thread at each side. Make a half knot in the thread close to the beads and place a blunt needle in it. Now position the fastener about 1cm (⅜ inch) from the knot.

2 Make a knot next to the fastener by working the short thread over the main thread and back through the loop. Tighten the knot. Repeat these knots down to the knot with the needle in it, making each one tight and even.

3 Work the end of the thread through the blunt needle and pull the needle through its knot. This will give you knots working in two different directions. Thread the end of the thread back down as many of the beads as you can. Cut off the end. Repeat on the other side when you have checked the positioning of the beads.

Dalmatian jasper and Thai silver bead necklace.

TOOLS AND MATERIALS

- Beading needle
- Blunt needle
- Fastener

SEE ALSO

⇨ FINDINGS PAGES 24–25

KNOTTING ONTO A FASTENER: USING GIMP

This is another method of knotting onto a fastener. In this example gimp has been used. In the past gimp was used for strengthening fragile threads when they were connected to fasteners. It is less necessary now, but can be used to change the look of the end of a piece. Gimp is a delicate material, so be careful when using it.

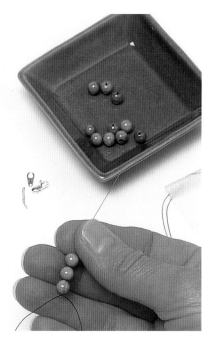

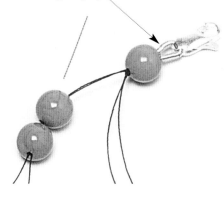

This method can also be used without adding the gimp.

1 Cut a good length of thread and two short lengths of gimp. Make a slip knot, or put a piece of tape on the far end of the thread and thread on three of the beads.

2 Thread carefully through the piece of gimp and work this on the thread through one side of the fastener. Make a knot, as you did in Knotting onto a Fastener (previous page) behind the first bead.

3 Thread back into the bead behind the knot and knot again. Thread through the next bead.

4 Remove the slip knot or tape and knot the two ends of thread together. Put some glue onto this knot, avoiding the beads, and trim the loose end.

TOOLS AND MATERIALS

- Gimp
- Masking tape (optional)
- Beading needle
- Fastener
- Blunt needle

5 Now thread on the rest of the beads. In this design bead caps have been used between the central beads. Finish with another piece of the gimp.

6 Work through the other side of the chosen fastener and bring the thread back through the last bead. Make sure that the tension of beads is correct, allowing for the knots that you will make between the beads to mirror the first side. Make a knot behind this bead.

7 Thread through the penultimate bead and make a knot. Then repeat this behind the third-from-last bead. Finish with another spot of glue on this knot, and work the thread back down the beads as far as you want to go. Trim the end.

Malachite necklace with bead caps.

SEE ALSO

⇨ KNOTTING ONTO A FASTENER PAGE 48

KNOTTING INTO A CLAMSHELL CALOTTE

Although the use of calottes is featured in Threading (see pages 36–37), the use of clamshell calottes to attach a fastener is slightly different because the beading thread is knotted through these findings.

Limestone and silver necklace.

2 Thread the other clamshell calotte. Make another double overhand knot and put a blunt needle into the knot. Draw the knot down towards the calotte, tightening it as it moves.

Open the loops sideways.

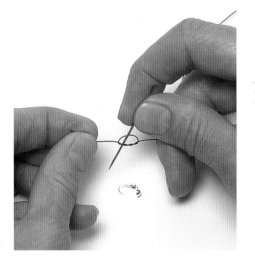

1 Cut a length of thread, allowing an extra 4–5cm (1 ½–2 inches) on each side for finishing. Make a secure knot in one end; a double overhand as shown in Knotting Between Beads (see page 53) will work well. Thread on the clamshell calotte. Trim the thread. Close the calotte over the knot – you can usually do this with your fingers and just use pliers for an extra squeeze. Thread on the beads.

3 Close the calotte over the knot as before. Gently roll the loops on the calottes over the loops on your chosen fastener.

TOOLS AND MATERIALS

- Clamshell calotte
- Round-nosed pliers
- Beading needle
- Blunt needle
- Fastener

SEE ALSO

⇨FINDINGS PAGES 24–25

Knotting between beads

Knots and decorative knotting are a way of extending design possibilities when working with beads. They can also be used to space beads evenly. Extend your techniques by studying books on Chinese knotting, macramé and braid making.

The type of knot you use will depend on the beads you use. Pearls, especially, are traditionally knotted because they can go on secreting enzymes that corrupt the threads.

Latvian amber bead necklace.

SINGLE OVERHAND KNOT

Simple overhand knots work well to space beads that have small holes.

Tweezers could also be used to move the knots.

Waxed thread or thread conditioner will help you to slide the knots.

1 Cut plenty of thread, allowing at least two-and-a-half times the length of your planned piece. Attach a fastener. Thread on the first bead, then make an overhand knot by wrapping the thread around your finger and taking the end back through the loop.

2 Put a strong blunt needle into this knot and slide the knot back towards the bead, using the needle to move the knot and your fingers to tighten it. Remove the needle as you tighten the knot. Continue in the same way, knotting between each bead and keeping the spacing and tension even by sliding the knots.

TOOLS AND MATERIALS
- Fastener
- Beading needle
- Blunt needle

DOUBLE OVERHAND KNOT

This technique gives a bulkier knot, for beads with slightly bigger holes. You will need to use more thread for this method.

Following the same principles as with the Single Overhand Knot (previous page), wrap the thread around your finger and thread into the loop twice instead of once. Control the knot with a blunt needle as before.

KNOTTING BETWEEN BEADS WITH A DOUBLE THREAD

This is another suggestion for knots to go between beads with reasonably large holes.

1 Allow approximately twice the length of the finished piece for each of the threads. Attach both threads onto a fastener and thread on the first bead. Make a reef knot behind the bead by working the threads left over right and through. Tighten this half of the knot. Now work right over left and through, and tighten again.

2 Add another bead and repeat the knot. You will find this much easier if you tape your piece to the worktop as you work. Continue in this way, thinking about tension as you work.

Reconstituted turquoise bead necklace.

SEE ALSO

⇨KNOTTING TO FINISH PAGES 46–51

KNOTTING TO SPACE BEADS

Knots can be used in the same way as French crimps to create spaces between beads.

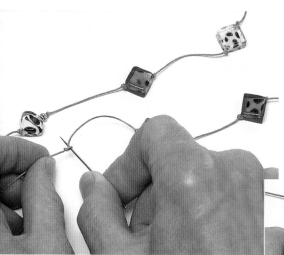

This method works in exactly the same way as usual knotting between beads, except that you use the blunt needle, or tweezers, to move the knots either apart, so that you create even spaces between the beads, or next to the bead. Use Single or Double Overhand Knots (see previous pages), depending on the width of the thread and the size of the holes in the beads. A measure can be used to space the beads if necessary.

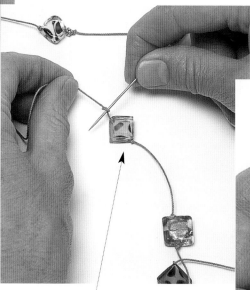

Randomly chosen and spaced Venetian beads.

Create a loop and bead fastener by knotting one bead on to sit sideways.

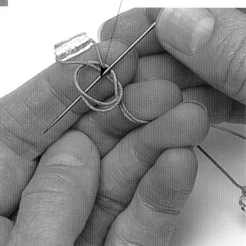

Working away from the centre is the easiest way to create these designs.

SEE ALSO

⇨SINGLE OVERHAND KNOT PAGE 52

⇨DOUBLE OVERHAND KNOT PAGE 53

⇨CRIMPING TO SPACE PAGE 41

Decorative knotting to finish

Strands of glass beads and Moroccan silver finished with half-knots.

The next few techniques are taken from macramé techniques and are excellent ways to transform a few beads into a complete necklace or bracelet.

These knotting techniques can also be used to finish multistrand pieces, by working half or square knots over all of the threads.

HALF-KNOTTING

This technique creates a naturally spiralling effect.

1 You need two working threads and a core thread. However, the core can be composed of as many threads as you like. Allow a long length for the two working threads. If you are attaching new thread (rather than knotting with some of the threads of a multistrand necklace), it is easiest to use one extremely long length and attach it from the middle. This strand is put into the last knot after the beads.

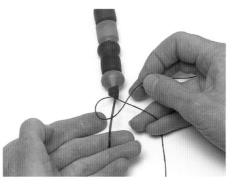

2 Take the left-hand thread under the middle and over the right-hand thread.

3 Take the right-hand thread back over the middle and under the left-hand thread. Pull the knot together.

4 Work on in the same way. The work will naturally spiral. You may find it easier to tape the piece to your worktop to help you regulate the tension.

SEE ALSO

⇨ SQUARE KNOTS PAGE 56

⇨ ADDING A "BUTTON" BEAD

AND BUTTONHOLING PAGE 57

BEADING TIP

Always allow plenty of thread so that you don't have to add more.

SQUARE KNOTS

A flat version of decorative knotting.

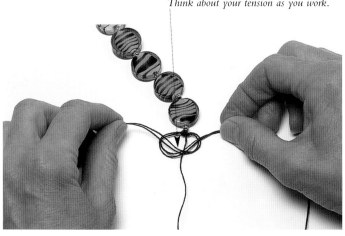

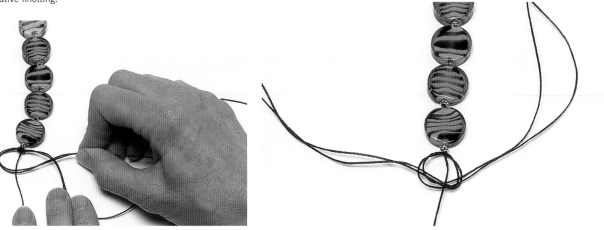

1 Add a good length of thread to the core thread. Double threads, as shown here, will give a more dramatic result. Take the left-hand threads under the middle and over the right-hand threads.

2 Take the right-hand threads back over the middle and under the left-hand thread. Pull the knot together.

Think about your tension as you work.

3 Now reverse the working threads, so take the left threads over the core and under the right threads. Then take the right-hand threads under the core and over the left threads. Continue in the same way, alternating the knots until you have reached the desired length.

Venetian glass beads and square knotting.

ADDING A "BUTTON" BEAD

As you near the end of your knotting, thread on a button or bead, then point the core threads back toward the centre of the piece. Continue to knot, working over these threads as well. Finish by using a needle to work in the loose ends and trim the ends.

Make your final knots as tight as possible.

Acrylic beads and half-knotting.

BUTTONHOLING

This will create a neat loop to go round your "button" bead.

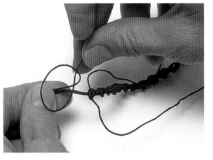

1 At the other side of the work, decide where your buttonhole should be and add another piece of thread to the core threads.

2 Make a loop above the core thread with the new thread. Bring the end under the core threads and back up through the loop. Pull this tight and continue in the same way until there is enough "buttonholing" for the button to pass through.

Check the size of your "buttonhole" carefully against your selected bead or button.

Make your last few knots as tight as possible.

3 Now turn this section back towards the centre of the piece.

4 Continue to knot over all of these threads. Finish off in the same way as the other side.

BEADS AND WIRE

Wires are a great resource for exciting designs. The range of materials you have at your disposal is wide, and wires are readily available in a variety of different gauges and finishes. There are many techniques to learn that combine beads and wire, all of which will help you to extend your design skills.

Drop earrings are quick and easy to make.

Drop earrings with findings

Making drop earrings using ready-made findings – eyepins or headpins – serves as a good introduction to working with wire. These findings consist of a length of wire finished with – in the case of the eyepin – a small loop at one end, or for the headpin a neat flat end, both of which support the beads. They are available in different lengths, and you should allow an extra 8mm (⁵⁄₁₆ inch) in length to finish off.

USING HEADPINS OR EYEPINS

For this example eyepins have been used and a selection of small beads complement the main bead.

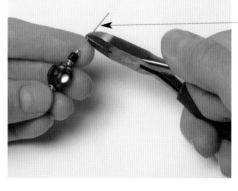

Headpins and eyepins come in hard and soft versions – use hard for earrings.

TOOLS AND MATERIALS

- Two eyepins
- Wire cutters
- Round-nosed pliers
- Two earwires

1 Thread the beads onto an eyepin. It is always a good idea to position a small bead at the bottom and top of the drop to ensure that the beads fit together well.

2 Use wire cutters to cut the excess wire at the top of the eyepin, ensuring there is 8mm (⁵⁄₁₆ inch) of wire left above the beads.

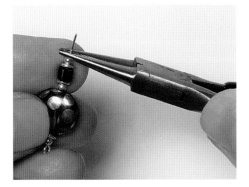

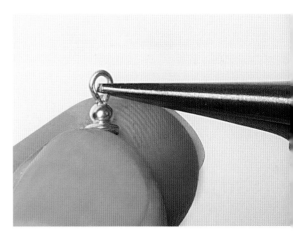

3 Hold the beads in place on the eyepin with the thumb and forefinger of one hand and use another finger to control the wire. Place round-nosed pliers directly above the beads and angle the wire towards you to 45 degrees.

4 Move the pliers to the top of the wire and, using their tips, roll the wire away from you to form a loop. If you can't do this in one movement, remove the pliers and put them back into the loop to give it another turn.

5 Neaten the loop, if necessary, by placing the pliers back into it.

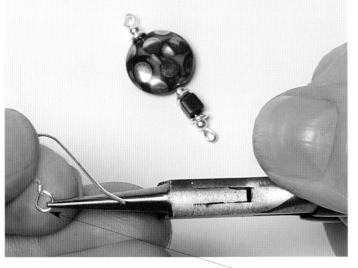

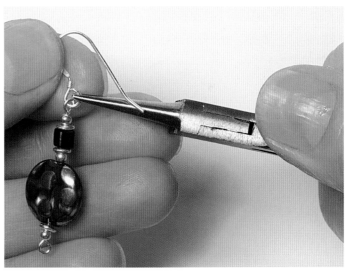

6 Take an earwire and use the pliers to open the loop sideways a little. Place the loop of the drop earring into the earwire loop.

Earwires come in many shapes and sizes. This is a fishhook earwire.

7 Use the pliers again to close up the earwire loop. Now make the second earring using the same techniques.

SEE ALSO

⇨FINDINGS PAGES 24–25

Drop earrings with wire

*Earrings with
simple loops.*

Drop earrings can be made from scratch using wire – instead of ready-made findings – by making loops in the wire to support the beads. The most suitable wires to work with are 0.6 or 0.8mm, although you can work with heavier or lighter gauges. You should consider the weight of your beads to assess the strength of wire you require. Also consider the strength of your hands, since heavier gauge wires, such as 1.0 or 1.2mm, can be difficult to work with. Always be generous with the amount of wire you work with, and while you practise forming loops, it is a good idea to work in copper or silver plate wire, which is inexpensive and easy to use. In the examples on the following pages 0.6mm silver plate wire was used.

SIMPLE LOOPS

Simple loops are obviously a good choice if you are new to working with wire, and they are perfectly adequate at securing a few beads on an earring.

The size of the loop is dependant on which part of the pliers is used. Here the tip is being used to make a very small loop.

1 Use wire cutters to cut two pieces of wire, allowing yourself plenty of length. Position round-nosed pliers about 5mm (³⁄₁₆ inch) from the end of one length of wire and use them to bend the wire toward you to 45 degrees.

2 Move the pliers to the top of the wire and, using their tips, roll the wire away from you to form a small, neat loop. If required, place the pliers back into the loop to neaten and centralize it.

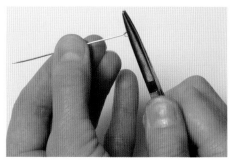

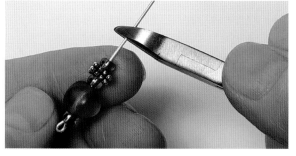

TOOLS AND MATERIALS
- Wire
- Wire cutters
- Pliers: round-nosed and flat-nosed
- Two earwires

3 Using flat-nosed pliers or your fingers, smooth down the wire a few times. This will strengthen and straighten it.

4 You can now thread on your chosen beads and finish the earring with another loop and an earwire, following Steps 2–7 of Drop Earrings with Findings on pages 58–59. Repeat to make the second earring.

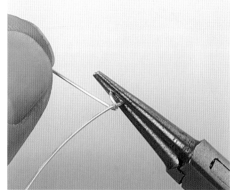

*A closed
loop section.*

INDIVIDUAL CLOSED LOOPS

These closed loops produce a very secure
and professional-looking finish.

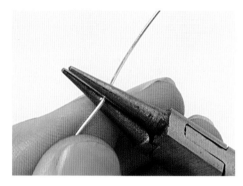

1 Cut two lengths of wire, allowing at least 6cm
(2 ½ inches) more than the length of your bead or
group of beads. Place round-nosed pliers onto the
wire and rotate them counterclockwise to create a
loop, allowing for a tail of excess wire to close the
loop with. You will need to experiment to create
the size of loop that is appropriate to the beads
you are using, and the length of wire you will
need to close the loop.

TOOLS AND MATERIALS

- Wire
- Wire cutters
- Pliers: round-nosed
  and flat-nosed
- Two earwires

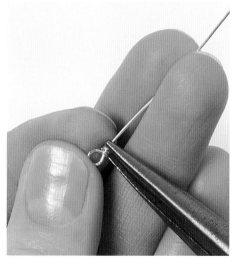

2 Hold the wire by placing the pliers across the loop
and use your finger and thumb to wind the tail
end of the wire around the wire beneath the loop.
You need to hold the wire firmly, but be careful
not to let the pliers mark it.

4 Use flat-nosed pliers to gently squeeze the sharp
end of the wire back into the coils you have just
formed. You have made a closed loop to secure
your beads.

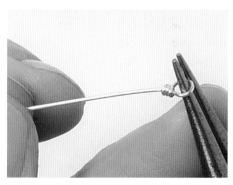

3 When you have wound the wire two or three
times, clip the excess off as neatly as you can
with wire cutters.

5 Put the round-nosed pliers back into the loop and
use your fingers to straighten the wire and
centralize the loop.

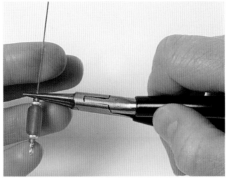

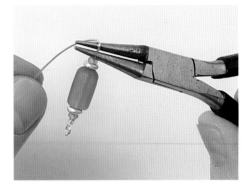

6 Thread on your chosen beads. It is always easier to work with a small bead next to a closed loop.

7 Place the round-nosed pliers across the wire next to the last bead and bend the wire towards you. You will learn to judge the length of the space that you are creating for the securing loops and to position the wire against the pliers accordingly.

8 Adjust the angle of the pliers to the wire, so that they are now sitting almost vertically to the beads, and use your finger and thumb to wind the wire back around the top arm of the pliers. You are aiming to form another loop to match the first one, with space to wind the wire underneath the loop to close it.

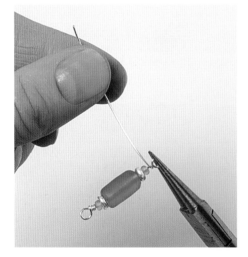

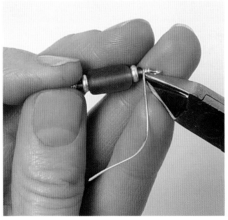

9 Holding the loop sideways with the pliers, use your other hand to wind the wire beneath the loop and back down towards the beads, to match the closed loop at the other end.

10 Use the wire cutters again to trim off the end of the wire.

11 Use the flat-nosed pliers to smooth the wire back against the beads.

SEE ALSO

⇨ FINDINGS PAGES 24–25

⇨ CLOSED-LOOP CHAIN PAGE 66

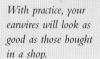

With practice, your earwires will look as good as those bought in a shop.

Making earwires

You can, of course, buy earwires to hang your drop earrings from, and there are many different types available from bead suppliers. However, it is also very satisfying to make your own. While it is a good idea to practise with cheaper wires, the final earwires should be made from sterling silver or gold wire, and 0.8mm or 0.6mm gauges.

SIMPLE EARWIRES

For this technique a hammer and block are optional.

You can wrap a small piece of fine wire above the loop to decorate the wire.

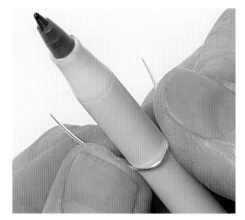

1 Cut two lengths of wire approximately 5cm (2 inches) long and bend them around a ballpoint pen, leaving slightly more length on one side.

2 Use round-nosed pliers to roll the shorter end back onto itself.

4 Clip off the extra length of wire on this side and smooth the end, which will go through the ear, with a cup bur or a small file.

3 Angle the other side of the wire a little, in line with the loop you have just made.

5 Hammer the rounded part of the earwire to give extra strength, if you wish. Repeat to make a second earwire.

TOOLS AND MATERIALS

- Wire
- Wire cutters
- Ball point pen
- Round-nosed pliers
- Cup bur or small file
- Hammer and block (optional)

Lapis and silver beads with "zig-zag" closed-loop earwires.

CLOSED-LOOP EARWIRES

This technique can be used with plain or decorative earwires.

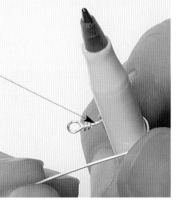

You could add a decorative bead above your closed loop to embellish the earwire.

1 Cut two lengths of wire approximately 6.5–7cm (2 ½–2 ¾ inches) long and make a closed loop at one end, following Steps 1–4 of Individual Closed Loops on pages 61–62. Curve both wires around a ballpoint pen, leaving slightly more length on the side without the closed loop.

TOOLS AND MATERIALS

- Wire
- Wire cutters
- Ball point pen
- Pliers: round-nosed and flat-nosed
- Cup bur or small file
- Hammer and block (optional)

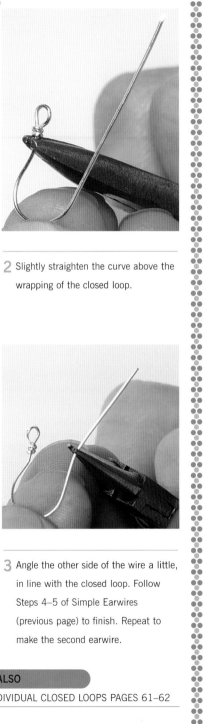

2 Slightly straighten the curve above the wrapping of the closed loop.

3 Angle the other side of the wire a little, in line with the closed loop. Follow Steps 4–5 of Simple Earwires (previous page) to finish. Repeat to make the second earwire.

SEE ALSO

⇨ INDIVIDUAL CLOSED LOOPS PAGES 61–62

Earrings on coil studs.

STUD EARRINGS

You can create stud earrings by gluing the appropriate findings onto the backs of suitable beads or cabochons, or you can use wire to create a few simple designs. Again you will want to use sterling silver or gold wire for the actual earrings, but it is useful to practise first with silver plate or copper wire.

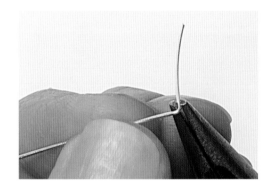

Coil studs

1 Cut two 10cm (4 inch) lengths of wire. Position flat-nosed pliers about 2cm (¾ inch) from the end of one length and make a right angle in the wire. Run your fingers or pliers along the longer length to strengthen it.

TOOLS AND MATERIALS

- Wire
- Wire cutters
- Pliers: round-nosed and flat-nosed
- Cup bur or small file
- Two scroll findings

Use good pliers with tiny ends to make neat loops.

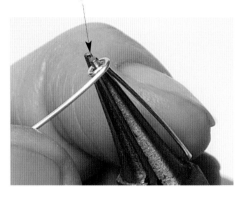

Try not to mark the wire with your pliers by holding too firmly.

2 Position the very end of a pair of round-nosed pliers against this angle, with the pliers sitting beside the shorter length of wire. Now roll the longer length around the tip of the pliers, so that you form a tiny spiral.

3 Hold the spiral with the flat-nosed pliers and carefully build up a small coil by winding the longer length of wire around the spiral with your fingers.

4 To hang a drop from the stud, cut the end of the wire you have been winding, leaving about 8mm (⁵⁄₁₆ inch). Use round-nosed pliers to roll the end into a loop and hang the drop from there.

6 Trim the wire that is at right angles to the stud, which will pass through the ear, to the required length and smooth the end with a cup bur or small file. To make the second stud, coil the wire in the opposite direction. Add scroll findings to the backs.

5 To add a bead onto the wire, thread the bead on then cut the excess wire, leaving about 5mm (³⁄₁₆ inch) below the bead, and finish with a tiny loop.

SEE ALSO
⇨SIMPLE LOOPS PAGE 60
⇨FINDINGS PAGES 24–25
⇨COILS PAGE 76

Closed-loop sections as pendants.

Chains and pendants

Another of the main uses for wire in bead jewellery is to make chains of beads, or to secure beads to form pendants. Closed loops are the key to these techniques and are used to create a chain of identical or coordinating sections.

CLOSED-LOOP CHAIN

By using closed loops you can create a chain of linked sections of beads that can't be pulled apart.

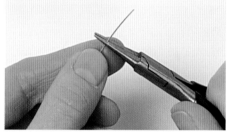

1 Cut two pieces of wire based on the length of your section of beads, plus 6cm (2 ½ inches) extra. Put one length to one side. Make the first section of the chain following the instructions for Individual Closed Loops on pages 61–62. Adjust the length of the other piece of wire that was kept as a measure and cut more lengths for the rest of the chain.

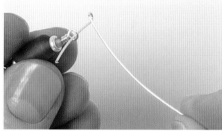

2 Form the first loop in another of these pieces and thread the beaded section that you have just made into this loop.

3 Wind the wire above this loop to secure it, clipping off and flattening in the end as usual.

4 Thread on the next set of beads, either in the same pattern or with variation, and finish this section as you did before.

5 Continue in the same way to complete the chain. Try to keep the loops reasonably loose to allow for natural movement: as you get more experienced, you will learn to angle the loops to make the chain hang well. Finish the chain by attaching a ready-made or self-made fastener, following the instructions on pages 69–72.

TOOLS AND MATERIALS
- Wire
- Wire cutters
- Pliers: round-nosed and flat-nosed

Closed-loop pendant on silver chain.

CLOSED-LOOP PENDANT

Before making the top loop you need to think about the choice of material from which the pendant will be hung.

WIRING TO HANG

You will often come across items, with holes that go from front to back, that you might like to hang flat as a pendant or as earrings.

A glass coin has been wired and threaded onto suede ribbon.

1 These can be made in exactly the same way as a drop earring (see page 61) or section of chain (see page 66). To alter the size of the loop, roll the wire around different parts of your pliers.

1 Cut a length of wire, being generous as always, and bend it through your pendant piece. You may want to decorate the front of the pendant with other beads.

2 Before closing the loop, thread the chain through it. Then wind the wire back down to the bead, ensuring that the fastener can't slip through the loop.

TOOLS AND MATERIALS

• Wire
• Wire cutters
• Pliers: round-nosed and flat-nosed

TOOLS AND MATERIALS

• Wire
• Wire cutters
• Pliers: round-nosed and flat-nosed
• Flat pendant piece with a hole in the centre

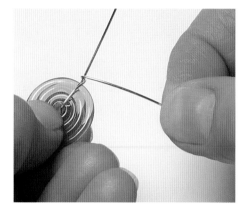

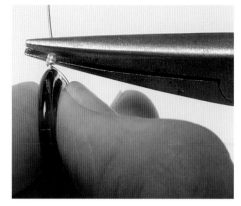

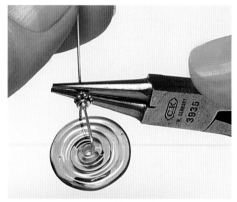

2 Wind one length of the wire around the other, above the pendant, two to three times, leaving some space to allow for movement.

The size of the loop will be determined by where you decide to wind the wire around your pliers.

3 Clip off the extra wire and flatten in the end with flat-nosed pliers.

4 Add a bead above this winding to make the pendant look more attractive and the wirework neater. Place round-nosed pliers horizontally above the bead and bend the wire towards you.

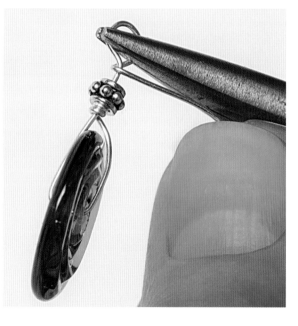

6 Wind the wire back down towards the bead, clip off the end and flatten it in again with flat-nosed pliers.

5 Adjust the angle of the pliers to the wire, so that they are now sitting almost vertically to the bead, and use your finger and thumb to wind the wire back around the top arm of the pliers. Think about the size of this loop, since you may want to thread something quite thick through it.

SEE ALSO

⇨ INDIVIDUAL CLOSED LOOPS PAGES 61–62

Indonesian glass beads on memory wire with a chain and ready-made fastener.

Fasteners and findings

Specialist suppliers provide a multitude of ready-made fasteners and findings that are easy to attach. Alternatively, since you have already learned how to make your own earwires, why not see how satisfying it is to be able to make your own fasteners and findings.

USING WIRE TO ATTACH A FASTENER

This method for fastening any necklace or bracelet combines a ready-made fastener and a length of chain.

Use plenty of wire.

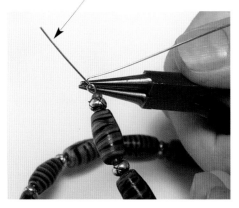

1 Attach a length of wire to the end of a necklace or the last section of a closed-loop chain with a closed loop (see page 61). Add a silver ball or a tiny bead. Position round-nosed pliers across the wire to ascertain the wrapping space and form a slightly larger loop above this.

2 Slide a ready-made fastener into this loop by opening it sideways.

The fastener can clip into the chain at any point to provide flexibility.

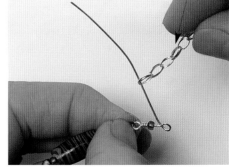

TOOLS AND MATERIALS

- Wire
- Wire cutters
- Tiny silver balls or matching beads
- Pliers: round-nosed and flat-nosed
- Ready-made fastener
- Length of chain

3 Wrap the wire back down to the bead, clip off the excess and flatten in the end with flat-nosed pliers, following the instructions for Individual Closed Loops on pages 61–62.

4 At the opposite end, repeat the whole process, sliding a length of chain into the loop instead of the fastener. If you prefer a more centralized fastening, you can add chain to both sides.

SIMPLE HOOKS

A plain hook and jump ring are the most simple fastener that you can make for a necklace.

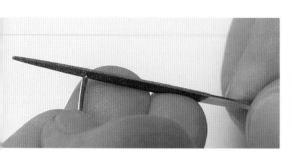

1 Cut about 5cm (2 inches) of wire and file one end.

2 Use round-nosed pliers to roll a neat loop at the smooth end.

You can decorate the hook with fine wire.

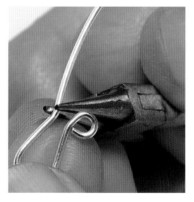

3 Bend the wire round the wider part of the pliers to create the hook shape.

4 Angle the wire a little, in line with the small loop. Clip off the excess wire and file this end. You can vary this loop by rolling back the second filed edge as well, or by winding a decoration of fine wire above the first loop.

TOOLS AND MATERIALS

- 1.0mm wire
- Wire cutters
- Cup bur or small file
- Pliers: round-nosed and flat-nosed

SEE ALSO
⇨SIMPLE LOOPS PAGE 60

JUMP RINGS

These are multipurpose findings that can be incorporated into many designs, and also make the ideal partner to the simple hooks.

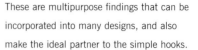

1 Cut a length of wire and wind it around one arm of a pair of round-nosed pliers, close to the base of the nose.

To make jump rings in other diameters wind the wire around different items.

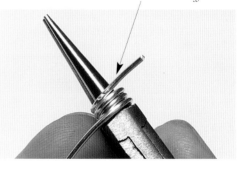

2 Repeat this a few times to make several jump rings.

TOOLS AND MATERIALS

- 1.0mm wire
- Wire cutters
- Pliers: round-nosed and flat-nosed
- Small file

3 Remove the coil from the pliers and use wire cutters to clip vertically through the coil to create a number of jump rings.

4 Open the jump rings sideways and file the inside edge if they need it. Always open them sideways when you want to add them into a design.

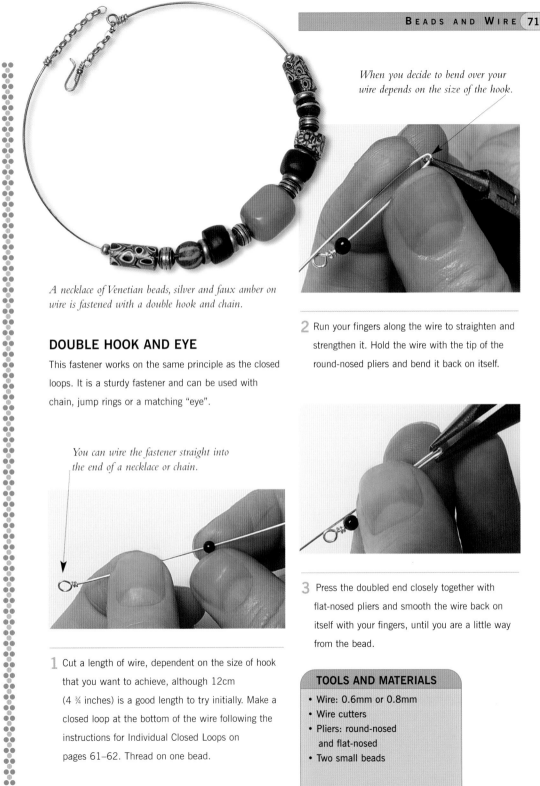

A necklace of Venetian beads, silver and faux amber on wire is fastened with a double hook and chain.

DOUBLE HOOK AND EYE

This fastener works on the same principle as the closed loops. It is a sturdy fastener and can be used with chain, jump rings or a matching "eye".

You can wire the fastener straight into the end of a necklace or chain.

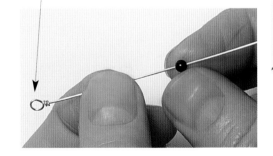

1 Cut a length of wire, dependent on the size of hook that you want to achieve, although 12cm (4 ¾ inches) is a good length to try initially. Make a closed loop at the bottom of the wire following the instructions for Individual Closed Loops on pages 61–62. Thread on one bead.

When you decide to bend over your wire depends on the size of the hook.

2 Run your fingers along the wire to straighten and strengthen it. Hold the wire with the tip of the round-nosed pliers and bend it back on itself.

3 Press the doubled end closely together with flat-nosed pliers and smooth the wire back on itself with your fingers, until you are a little way from the bead.

TOOLS AND MATERIALS

- Wire: 0.6mm or 0.8mm
- Wire cutters
- Pliers: round-nosed and flat-nosed
- Two small beads

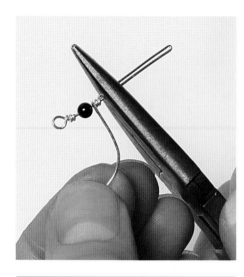

4 Still holding the doubled wire firmly in the pliers, make a right angle with the remaining length of wire. Wind this length of wire back down to the bead. Clip the extra length and flatten the end.

Practise making different sizes of hooks.

5 Bend the doubled wire around the pliers to create a hook shape.

6 Angle the doubled wire a little, in line with the closed loop.

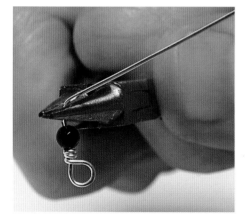

Try to match the size of the "eye" to the hook.

9 Hold these loops gently with the pliers and wind the wire back down towards the bead. Clip off the excess length and flatten the end in with flat-nosed pliers.

7 To make the eye, repeat the first step with a similar length of wire, then place the pliers horizontally across the wire above the bead and bend the wire towards you.

8 Adjust the angle of the pliers to the wire and wind the wire around the lower arm twice.

SEE ALSO

⇨ INDIVIDUAL CLOSED LOOPS PAGES 61–62

Wrapping beads

Recycled glass bead wrapped with wire and beads.

Extending your use of wires can greatly increase your jewellery-making potential. By learning to decorate beads with wire, you can add your own originality to plain beads, or create something very special from one feature bead.

WRAPPING INDIVIDUAL BEADS

This is an easy way to embellish a plain bead, using wires and a few other beads.

1 Cut a length of 0.8mm wire about three times the length of your bead. Make a closed loop at one end following the instructions for Individual Closed Loops on pages 61–62. Now cut a long length of 0.6mm wire, in the example shown it is 12 times the length of the bead. Use the round-nosed pliers to make a tiny spiral at the end of this length.

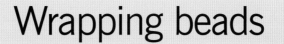

2 Slide the spiral over the thicker wire and thread both of them into the bead, from what will be the bottom, if possible, so that the spiral fits inside the hole in the bead.

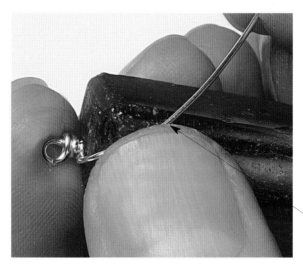

3 Holding everything very firmly in your hand, start to wrap the 0.6mm wire around the bead. When you have made one wrap, thread some of the small beads onto the wire and continue to wrap, spacing the beads into the wraps as you work.

Hold and wrap as tightly as you can.

TOOLS AND MATERIALS

- Wire: 0.8mm and 0.6mm
- Wire cutters
- Pliers: round-nosed and flat-nosed

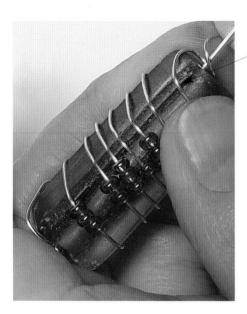

Try to keep the positioning in place as you wrap the wire.

4 When you reach the top of the bead, wrap the wire as firmly around the bead as possible, then move it back onto the thicker wire and wind around this a few times. Clip off the extra length and flatten in the end.

5 Push this spiral as close into the bead as you can, then add another bead to the 0.8mm wire and make a closed loop above it. Trim the wire and flatten in the end.

6 To tighten the wire around the beads, use the tips of flat-nosed pliers against the wire and turn each wrap to make an angle in the wire. Do this as many times as you like, making sure you use the pliers carefully so that they don't damage the bead or the wire. Be careful not to over tighten to the extent that the wire snaps.

WIRE ON WIRE WRAPPING

Wrapping with two different wires will create other decorative results.

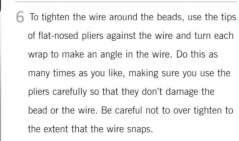

Wrap the contrast wire very closely or with spaces to create different effects.

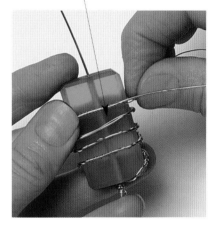

Start in the same way as for Wrapping Individual Beads on pages 73–74, but attach a third, longer length of finer wire to the wrapping wire. Wrap this around the main wrapping wire as you wind up the main bead. Finish off in the same way as before, angling the wire if you wish.

MATERIALS

- Wire: 0.8mm, 0.6mm and a finer wire
- Wire cutters
- Pliers: round-nosed and flat-nosed

WRAPPING GROUPS OF BEADS

This is an attractive way to enhance a bracelet or group of beads within a chain, and would also enhance a single strand of beads. In the example we have used two lengths of memory wire and put some spacer bars between the beads.

1 Thread the beads onto memory wire following the instructions for Threading on page 40. Connect the two strands with spacer bars, threading them in with the beads, then put a single link of chain on one side of the bracelet and a small length of chain on the other side. Cut a good length of 0.6mm wire and wind it around the base of the loop of one of the pieces of memory wire.

MATERIALS
- Memory wire
- 0.6mm wire
- Wire cutters
- Pliers: round-nosed and flat-nosed

Position the small beads where they will sit neatly.

2 Start to wrap the wire around both strands of beads. As you continue to wrap, add in smaller beads on the fine wire.

3 Finish by winding the end of the wrapping wire very tightly above one of the memory wire loops. Clip the end of the wire and flatten it in with the flat-nosed pliers.

Amethyst quartz and silver beads are wrapped with silver wire and smaller amethyst quartz beads.

4 Add a fastener to the single link of chain, following the instructions for Using Wire to Attach a Fastener on page 69.

SEE ALSO
⇨THREADING PAGE 40
⇨FINDINGS PAGES 24–25
⇨USING WIRE TO ATTACH A FASTENER PAGE 69

Decorations and spacers

Earrings with coil decorations and spacers.

When making drop earrings or chains of beads, decorative wire and spacers between beads extend the versatility of the work. They can be made with many different types of wire, and used in different ways. A simple coil or triangle shape can be used as a variation at the bottom of drop earrings. Spacers can be made with simple loops if they are intended for use in earrings, but if they are to be incorporated into chains, closed loops at either end are preferable.

COILS

These can be used as decorative headpins for drop earrings or incorporated into other designs.

A larger loop in the centre will create a different look.

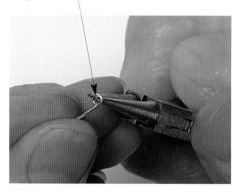

2 Position the flat-nosed pliers across the loop to hold it firmly, but without marking the wire. Use your fingers to wind the length of wire around the loop to create a coil.

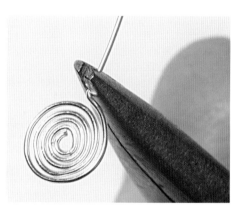

3 Position the pliers against the finished coil to re-angle the wire.

1 Cut a length of wire and make a tiny loop with the smallest point of the round-nosed pliers.

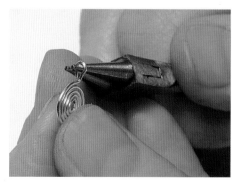

4 The coil can be finished with a simple loop, as shown here, or a closed loop.

TOOLS AND MATERIALS
- Wire
- Wire cutters
- Pliers: round-nosed and flat-nosed

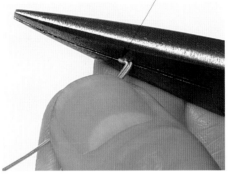

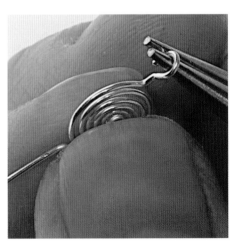

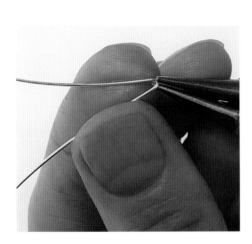

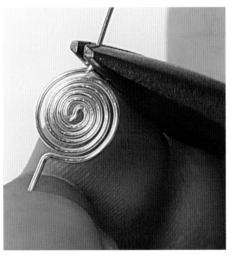

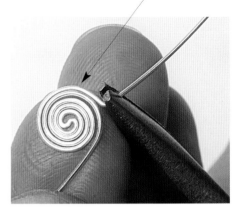

COIL SPACERS

Coils can be formed to be worked between other elements of a design.

Forming the coil is difficult and needs to be done with lots of small movements.

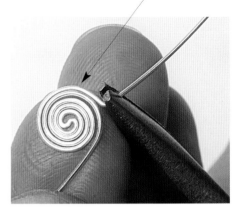

Make sure that the coil doesn't become too big or it will start to lose shape and strength.

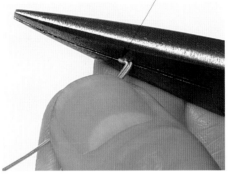

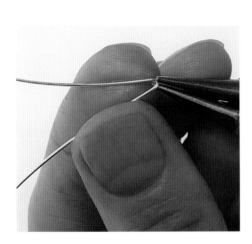

1 Cut two lengths of wire and put one aside to be used as a measure. For the example shown 15cm (6 inches) of wire has been cut. Position round-nosed pliers on the wire just off centre and turn the wire back onto itself. Squeeze the two sides together.

2 Hold firmly with flat-nosed pliers, and with the longer length of wire on the inside, gently start to form a coil.

3 When you have reached the required size of coil, turn the outside length of wire to 90 degrees.

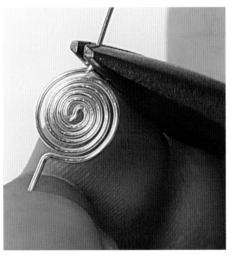

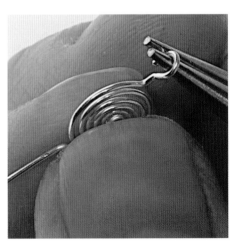

4 Continue to wind the other length until it is opposite the first, then turn this to 90 degrees as well.

5 The ends can be cut to about 6mm (¼ inch) to be finished with a simple loop, or cut to about 3cm (1 ¼ inches) to be completed with a closed loop.

TOOLS AND MATERIALS
- Wire
- Wire cutters
- Pliers: round-nosed and flat-nosed

ZIGZAG SPACERS

Zigzag spacers work well in either earrings or necklaces. This is an excellent design with which to experiment with hammering. Ideally you need a small block to hammer onto, and you need a small hammer, but it is fine to experiment with household tools and smooth surfaces. If you are using coloured or plated wires the surface can be damaged by hammering, although this could be a feature of the design. In the example below we have used 1.0mm copper wire.

Copper wire zigzag spacers between furnace beads on closed loop sections.

Keep the design quite simple so that it is easy to reproduce it many times.

1 Cut two lengths of wire and put one aside to be used as a measure. In this example the wire is 9cm (3 ½ inches) long. Make sure that the end has a neat cut, then make a loop at the end around round-nosed pliers.

2 Move the pliers along a little further and turn the wire back onto itself.

4 At the end of the zigzag, make a final turn back so that you create a loop that turns back towards the spacer piece. Clip off the excess wire.

3 Continue to turn the wire in the same way so it zigzags from side to side. You can vary the length between bends to make a pleasing shape.

5 Hammer the spacer, if desired, to give extra strength. This will slightly increase its size, so you may want to re-scale your design before making more. Now that you know the length of wire required, you can cut more and repeat the steps until you have enough spacers for your design. If you want uniformity in your design, you may make your spacers on a jig (see page 79). The spacers can be linked with simple or closed loops or jump rings.

TOOLS AND MATERIALS
- Wire
- Wire cutters
- Pliers: round-nosed and flat-nosed
- Hammer and block (optional)

SEE ALSO
⇨ SIMPLE LOOPS PAGE 60
⇨ INDIVIDUAL CLOSED LOOPS PAGES 61–62
⇨ JUMP RINGS PAGES 70–71
⇨ USING A JIG PAGE 79

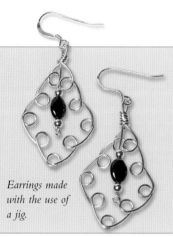

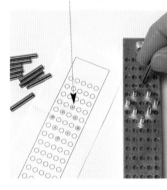

Earrings made with the use of a jig.

Using a jig

A jig is a great tool which was created by a jewellery designer to help jewellery makers achieve uniformity when using wires. A jig is a base plate with a number of holes in it. Into these holes movable pegs can be placed in a range of patterns. The wire is then wound around and between the pegs, creating uniform pieces for earrings, pendants or spacers. The movement of the wire around the pegs also strengthens the wire. Using a jig takes some practice, but once the technique is mastered, a jig pattern can make repeating designs that are much easier to create.

Make a record of your design so you can keep it.
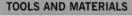

1 Set up the jig by placing the pegs in the holes, as shown in the pattern. Cut 30cm (12 inches) of wire for this example. Push 5cm (2 inches) of wire into the hole above the first peg, to create a firm start for the pattern.

2 Wind the wire around each of the pegs, as firmly as possible, pressing the loops down if you need to. Use a cup bur or knitting needle to help. Continue until you reach the end of the jig pattern.

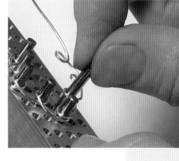

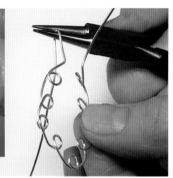

3 Take the wire off the jig by removing the pegs or gently lifting the wire off the pegs. To make this particular design into an earring, bend one end of the wire so it reaches above the top loop a little, then use round-nosed pliers to bend it back down so it passes through the centre of the earring. Wind the other end of wire round the base of the loop, following the instructions for Individual Closed Loops on pages 61–62.

4 Add beads to the central wire, clip the length and make a tiny loop at the bottom to hold the beads in place. Attach an earwire to the top loop and repeat to make a second earring.

TOOLS AND MATERIALS

- A jig and pegs
- Wire
- Wire cutters
- Cup bur or knitting needle
- Pliers: round-nosed and flat-nosed

SEE ALSO

⇨ INDIVIDUAL CLOSED LOOPS PAGES 61–62

⇨ SIMPLE LOOPS PAGE 60

⇨ FINDINGS PAGES 24–25

Knitting with wire

The use of beads when knitting adds wonderful texture and colour to wire.

Knitting with wire is a great way of making jewellery, and all you need is some wire, beads and knitting needles. The great thing about this technique is that you only need to learn casting on, garter stitch and casting off.

Choosing a wire

Normally, a 0.3 or 0.2mm (28 or 32) gauge wire is best for knitting, but wire does vary between manufacturers. Work a small practice piece to test if your wire is suitable for knitting. If it is too fine, the wire will snap; too thick and it will be impossible to knit with.

Getting the tension right

Knitting with wire is at first a strange experience, especially if you are an accomplished knitter who uses a firm tension. You are unable to pull the tension up with wire, so it has to be correct from the start. The wire has to be kept quite "loopy" on the needles to enable the needles to form the stitches. When you first start to knit, your work will appear to be a tangled mess. Don't worry: this is normal and it will need to be pulled into shape, which is when it comes to life.

Add beads directly onto the spool. The wire is not cut at this point.

1 Start by threading the number of beads you need onto the beading wire without cutting it. Keep pushing the beads down towards the spool end of the wire.

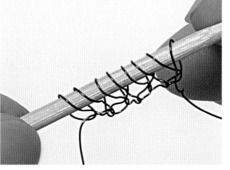

2 Cast on eight stitches. This will look like quite a jumbled mess. You may also find it necessary to cast on three or four times until you get the hang of working with wire, which is quite a good exercise since your tension will improve each time.

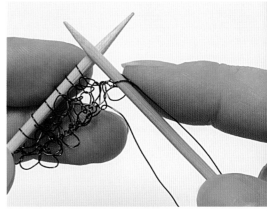

3 Start by knitting three plain rows in order to leave some space between the knitting needles and the beads you are about to knit with.

TOOLS AND MATERIALS

- Beading wire
- Bamboo knitting needles
- Cutting pliers

Keep the tension loose.

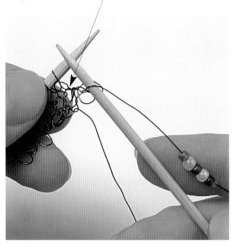

The bead is now ready to be knitted into the wire.

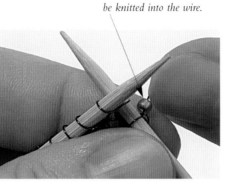

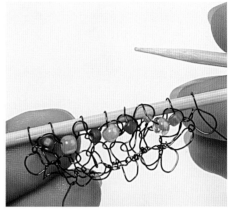

4 Knit the first stitch of Row 4 as normal. Push some beads up from the base of the wire so that you are holding a few in the palm of your dominant hand.

5 Push a bead up to the back of the needles, then knit the second stitch, which knits the bead into the stitch.

6 Continue along the row, knitting a bead into each stitch, except the last stitch, which is knitted without a bead: if you were to include a bead in the last stitch it would stick out through the side of the work and look out of place.

Don't be afraid to pull the knitting into shape.

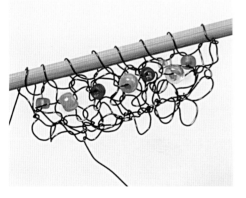

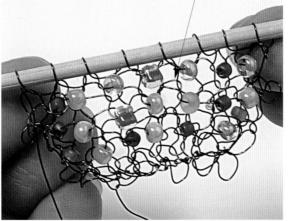

8 Row 6: knit a bead into all the stitches except the first and last stitch. Continue alternating from a knit row and a bead row until your work has reached the required length. Cast off in the normal manner. To finish the wire ends off simply wind the wire around itself to secure, making sure there are no sharp edges sticking out.

7 Row 5: knit a plain row without beads; this will make the beads go further and give you one smooth flat side that is more comfortable next to the skin.

SEE ALSO

⇨CROCHETING WITH WIRE PAGES 84–85

French knitting with wire

Three French knitted wire tubes, twisted to form a necklace.

This technique will transport most of us back to our childhood, and you can still obtain children's versions of the knitting spool, the tool often referred to as a knitting Nancy. It is possible to make your own spool knitter: just hammer four large nails into a wooden cotton reel (if you can locate one) in a circle, so the nails are equidistant to each other. Modern-day equivalents – even a mechanical version – are also available to buy. The knitting spool used for the following examples has five pegs, but the technique is still very much the same.

As with knitting with wire, beads can be added at any time. It's best to thread them onto the wire before you start to knit, then as you begin to work you can just thread them through the wire between the pegs. As you work each stitch they will disappear down the centre of the spool to form the "tube".

There is a definite knack to this technique, so don't be put off by the first few attempts, and keep practising.

Choosing a wire

Usually either a 0.3 or 0.2mm (28 or 32) gauge wire works well, but experiment with the various gauges to see which works best for you. Success depends on how much you pull the wire and whether the wire will break under the strain. Wire gauges do vary between manufacturers, so it's well worth making several samples.

1 If you plan to use beads, start by threading the amount you need onto the beading wire without cutting it. Keep pushing the beads down towards the spool end of the wire. Insert the loose end of the wire down through the centre of the spool, then bend the wire up over the base of the spool to secure it.

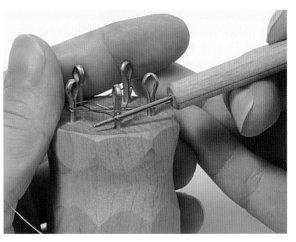

TOOLS AND MATERIALS
- 0.3mm/0.2mm wire
- French knitting tool and stylus (or needle if you have made your own spool)
- Cutting pliers

2 Wrap the working end of the wire so that it forms a star pattern around the pegs.

3 Working counterclockwise, place the wire against the next peg along, above where the initial wrap of wire sits. Place the stylus – or a knitting needle – if you have made your own knitting spool, from the top through the initial, lower loop of wire.

Make sure the lower wire doesn't come over the top as well.

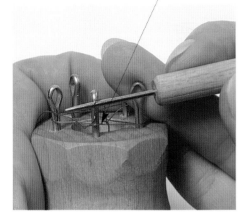

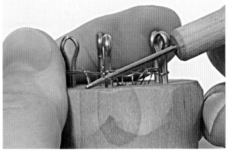

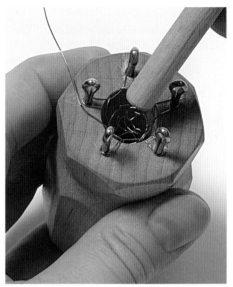

4 Carefully lift the loop over the working wire, then over the peg. Give the wire end at the base of the spool a gentle tug.

5 Lay the working wire across the top half of the next peg along then, as before, place the stylus through the initial loop and lift it over the wire then the peg. Continue in the same way, remembering to give a tug on the wire end after every one or two stitches.

6 When you have completed two or more rows, turn the stylus on its end and gently push the wire rows into the centre of the spool. This encourages the stitches to travel downwards since wire does not fall and droop as thread would normally do.

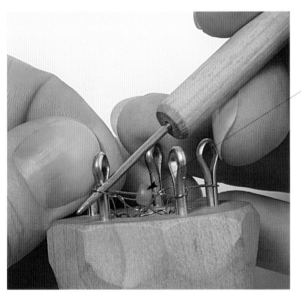

There should be enough room to lift the loop if the bead is laid on the wire between the two pegs.

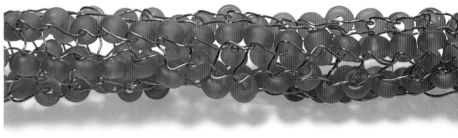

7 If you are using beads, simply bring a bead up from the base of the wire reel and where you position the wire from peg to peg. If you prefer not to knit with beads, you can always fill the tubes with beads, provided they are large enough not to fall out.

8 To finish, cut the working wire, leaving about a 30cm (12 inch) tail. Then, as you remove each loop in turn from the pegs, thread the wire end through the loop to stop the tube unravelling. The finished tube can be used as the base of a necklace or bracelet.

SEE ALSO

⇨KNITTING WITH WIRE PAGES 80–81

Crocheting with wire

Crocheting with wire and beads is great fun but, unlike thread, wire does not stretch and can be very unforgiving. You may well need to work on your tension until you are able to keep the wire just loose enough to move the crochet hook through the links. You can also experiment to see how different effects can be achieved using varying sizes and shapes of beads.

Simple beaded wire crochet chains.

Choosing a wire

You will need to experiment with different types and gauges of wire, although 0.2 and 0.16mm (32 and 34) gauges seem to work best.

1 Unravel a short length of wire from the reel, about 15cm (6 inches). If you want to crochet with beads, thread on the required amount of beads for your project, pushing them towards the reel. Hold the crochet hook in your right hand and lay the wire across the hook, wrapping it around it to form a loop. Twist the end of the wire around the base of the loop to secure, leaving a short end.

TOOLS AND MATERIALS
- 0.2mm/0.16mm wire
- Large crochet hook
- Cutting pliers

Hold the wire securely between the thumb and middle finger to encourage the chain downwards and prevent overtightening.

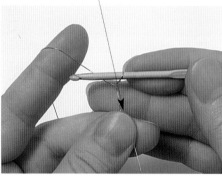

2 Keeping the hook in your right hand, and holding the base of the loop between your thumb and middle finger, wrap the long, working end of the wire around the little finger on your left hand and drape it over the back of the hand, supporting it with the first finger.

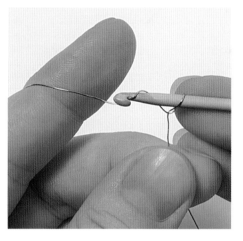

3 Holding the base of the loop on the hook with the thumb and middle finger of the left hand, insert the hook under the wire and draw back through the loop.

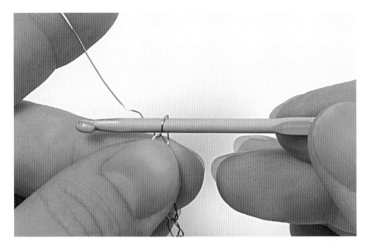

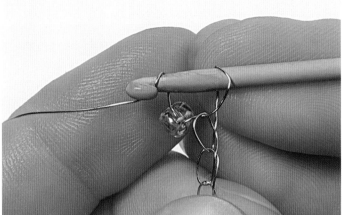

4 Continue in the same manner, releasing the wire through the fingers, until the chain reaches the required length. A rhythm will soon start to appear.

5 To include beads, move several beads up onto the length of wire draped over your first finger, and adjacent to the hook. Separate one bead and move it into a position close to the last loop you have crocheted.

Each bead is captured between the length of the wire and where the crochet hook is inserted around the wire.

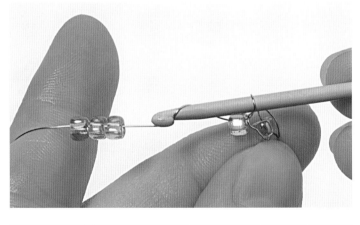

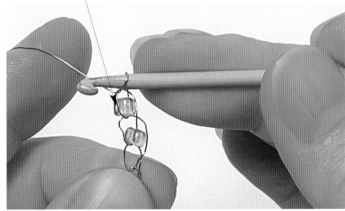

6 Insert the hook under the wire beyond the bead and pull through.

7 Continue in the same way, inserting one bead into each link formed.

Gently "tweak" the stitches to make sure each bead is sitting within each chain link.

BEAD LOOM TECHNIQUES

Beadwork refers to the techniques that usually involve weaving small glass beads onto thread. Beadweaving can be achieved either freehand (see pages 98–129) or using a bead loom. These techniques are long established in history, in many different parts of the world, especially amongst indigenous Americans and a variety of African societies.

Using a bead loom

It is worth investing in a good loom if you enjoy working with one.

When using a loom, you can either work "freehand", designing as you work, or you can draw a graph first and follow it as you would an embroidery pattern.

In most cases it's better to work with an odd number of beads in each row. This gives more scope for patterns, and allows for making integral buttonholes. Whichever way you work, it is important to always allow plenty of thread, and leave long ends when you need to add more thread so that you can weave them back into the work.

Getting started

Looming can be done on a purpose-made loom or on a very simple structure featuring parallel nails in a wooden rectangle. You'll also need small beads, very fine, strong synthetic thread and fine beading needles. A special, readily available, needle that has an "eye" running through the length of it is very useful. You may also choose to wax the threads as you work.

TOOLS AND MATERIALS

- Synthetic thread
- Beading needles
- Wooden or plastic loom
- A strong blunt needle

THREADING A LOOM

Follow the following instructions to set up your loom, always allowing plenty of thread and positioning the warp threads carefully.

1 Cut one more warp (lengthwise) thread than the number of beads you need for your design and allow for double threads for the outside edges. For example, if you want to create a piece with nine beads across the row, use 12 warp threads. Allow plenty of extra length to attach the warp threads to the loom.

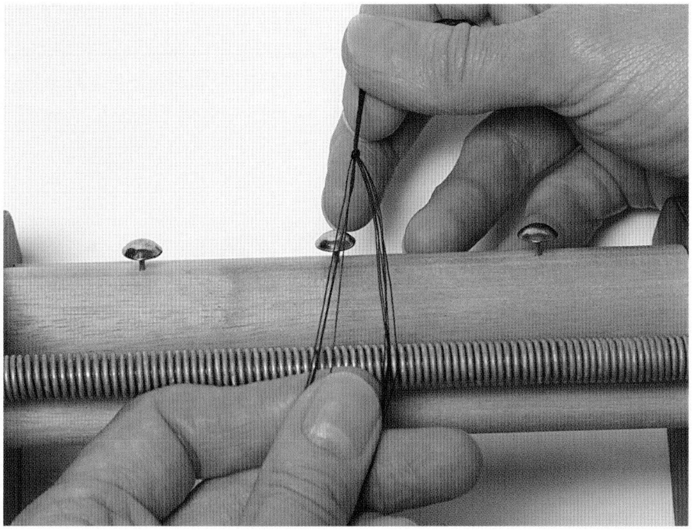

2 Knot the threads together at one end and position the knot over a peg on the loom. If you want to weave a piece that is longer than your loom, wind the extra length around the loom at the end that is furthest away from you.

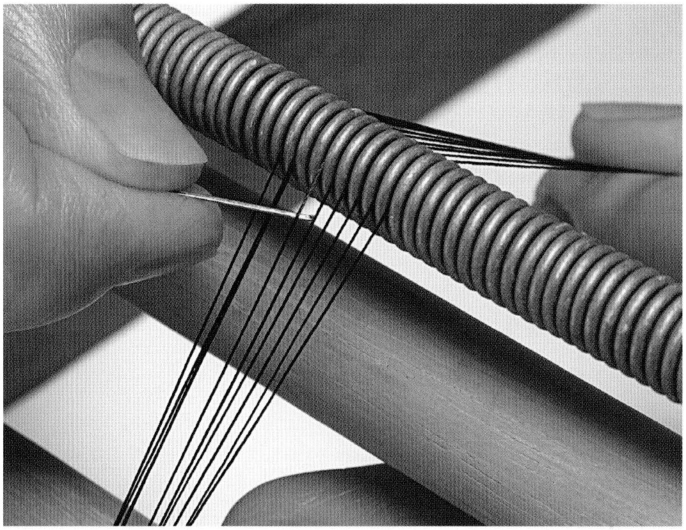

3 Start to position the threads in the grooves of the loom with the help of a needle.

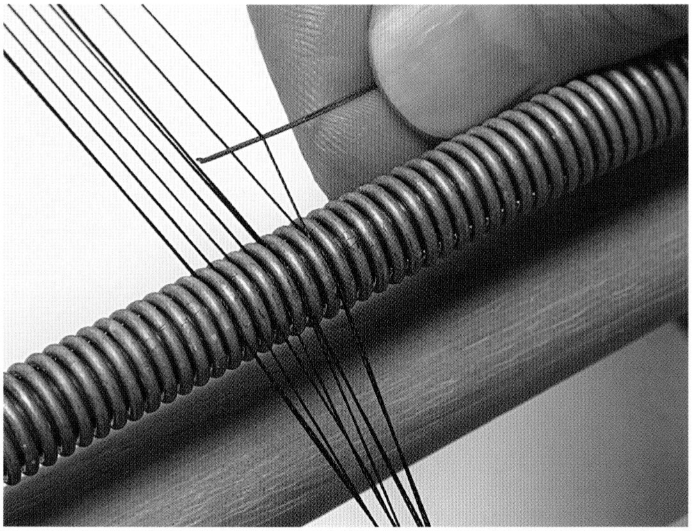

4 Repeat the positioning at the end closest to you, putting the threads into the slots that face each other.

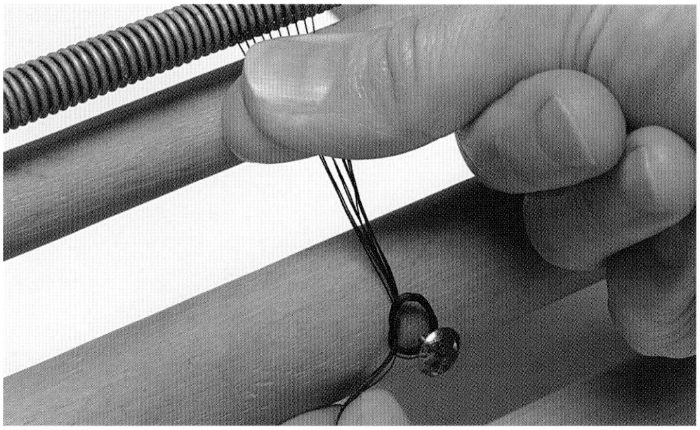

5 Tie these threads onto the peg at this end of the loom. Now adjust the nuts on the loom so that the threads are as taut as possible.

SEE ALSO
⇨TOOLS PAGE 10–13
⇨THREADS PAGES 14–17

WEAVING ON A LOOM

Very small beads such as rocailles, delicas and seed beads (see page 20) are usually used on the loom. Delicas are especially good for weaving and loomwork because they are the most uniform in size and quality. Other beads will vary in size within the different categories, so you should decide whether or not you are happy with this for your end result.

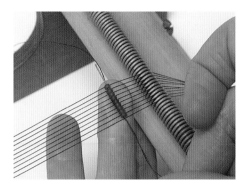

2 Holding them in place with your finger, bring the thread back through the beads, making sure that you go above the warp threads this time. You may find it easier to change the position of the loom as you do this.

Leave a fairly long end and add new thread when you need more to weave with.

4 If you are working on a long piece of loomwork, loosen the loom and wind the work towards you, releasing the extra length on the warp threads.

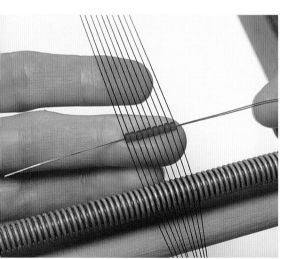

1 Thread another length of thread onto the beading needle ready for weaving, allowing plenty so that you do not have to make too many joins in your work. Pick up the beads for the first row on the needle. Position the beads under the loom, pressing them up between the warp threads, and bring your weaving thread through.

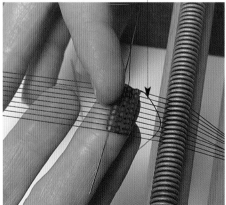

3 Work on along the warp threads, changing colours or design as you want to, and adding new weaving threads as you need them. Push the rows of weaving back together as you work to keep everything as tight and neat as possible.

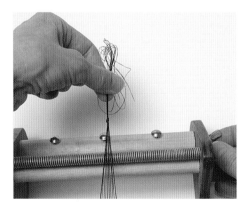

5 When you have reached the desired length, loosen the tension on the loom and lift the work off.

Finishing the loomwork

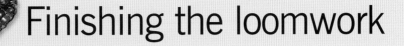

An integrated buttonhole.

Finishing the loomwork and creating fasteners is the most difficult aspect of using a loom. You need to deal with the warp threads and any additional weaving threads in the piece, and create a fastener. Some of the methods of fastening are created when the looming is finished; others are an integral part of the work.

TIDYING THE THREADS

When finishing any loomwork, first deal with the ends of the weaving threads.

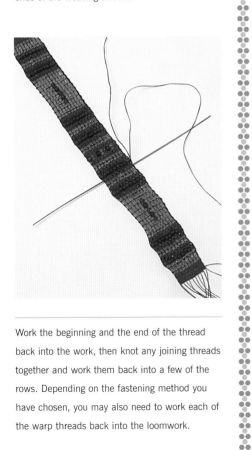

Work the beginning and the end of the thread back into the work, then knot any joining threads together and work them back into a few of the rows. Depending on the fastening method you have chosen, you may also need to work each of the warp threads back into the loomwork.

BACKING THE WEAVING

One of the easiest ways to complete the work is to back it with a piece of ribbon, or something similar.

1 Position the beading strip on the backing strip. In this instance you can loosely knot the ends of the warp threads together and fold them between the two strips.

A better look will be achieved by using the same width of backing and weaving.

2 Use a sewing needle and sewing thread in a colour that is close to the beading and backing to sew the loomed piece to the backing strip.

SEE ALSO

⇨THREADS PAGES 14–17

PLAITING THE ENDS

This is an easy way for children to finish loomed pieces.

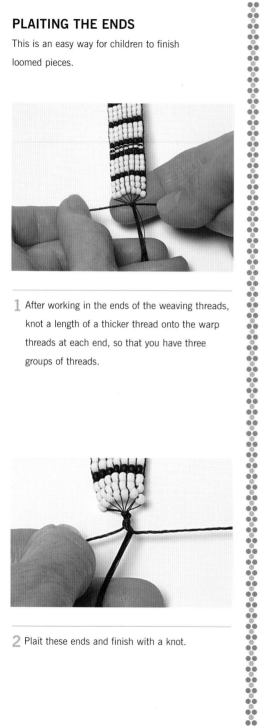

1 After working in the ends of the weaving threads, knot a length of a thicker thread onto the warp threads at each end, so that you have three groups of threads.

2 Plait these ends and finish with a knot.

BUTTONS AND LOOPS

This method of finishing involves attaching fasteners to and making loops with the warp threads. You can use actual buttons, or choose beads that will work as a fastener. You can use as many loops and buttons as you like, depending on the width of your work.

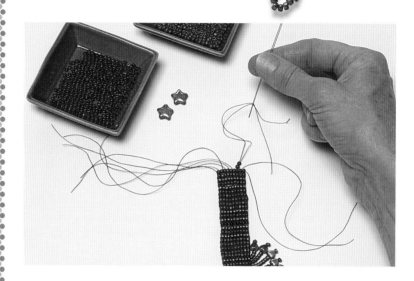

1 When you have finished the looming and worked the weaving threads back into the work, you can attach the buttons at one end. Select two warp threads at one side, and using a beading needle thread on two small beads.

2 Now thread on the button – either an actual button or a larger bead used as a button as here – and add another small bead. Thread back into the button and back into the two small beads beneath it. The small bead at the other side will hold everything in place.

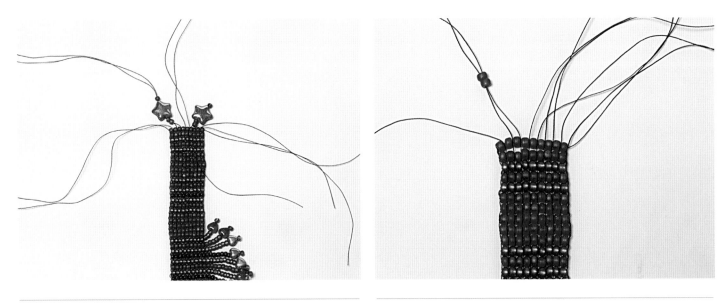

3 Knot these two threads together under the small beads for extra security. Now add the second button, if required.

4 At the other end of the work, select the corresponding warp threads and thread on two small beads.

Make sure that the tension on the weaving is good before you finish off the ends.

6 Check that the loop is large enough for the button to pass through, but not too large. Then work both threads back through the two small beads. Knot these ends for security. Finish by working in the threads.

5 Separate the threads and add more small beads to each side. Cross the threads and thread back down the other side of the loop.

SEE ALSO

⇨ TIDYING THE THREADS PAGE 89

INTEGRATED BUTTONHOLES

This method of finishing involves planning before you start the work. First choose either a button or a suitable bead and ascertain the length of buttonhole you require. Alternatively, you can weave a tab on the loom to pass through the buttonhole.

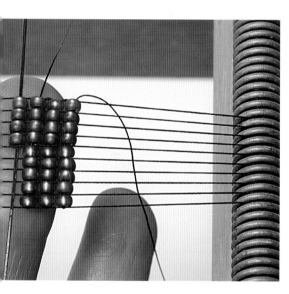

Making the buttonhole

1 Thread an odd number of beads on the loom (so that you can leave a gap of one bead for the buttonhole, and work a few rows to begin the piece) before starting to work the buttonhole. If there are nine beads in the row, thread on four beads in the next row and bring the needle out in the middle of the warp threads.

LOOMING TIP

Use wax or thread conditioner if your thread needs help in moving smoothly.

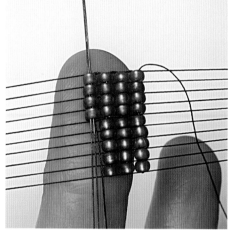

2 Work back through these beads.

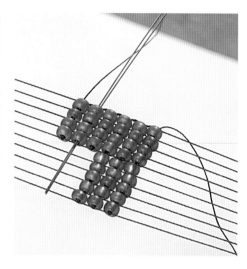

3 Continue in this way until you have worked enough rows to create one side of a hole that your chosen button or bead will fit through. Now work back down these rows so that you can start again on the other side of the buttonhole.

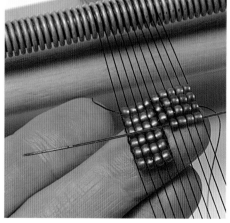

4 Turn the loom around and repeat Steps 1–3 on the other side of the loom, leaving a space between the central warp threads.

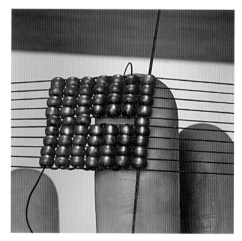

5 Continue to work across the full width of the loom to complete the buttonhole and progress with the work.

6 When you have finished, lift the piece off the loom and work the weaving threads back into the beadwork. Starting at the end where you have made the buttonhole, work each of the warp threads back into the looming.

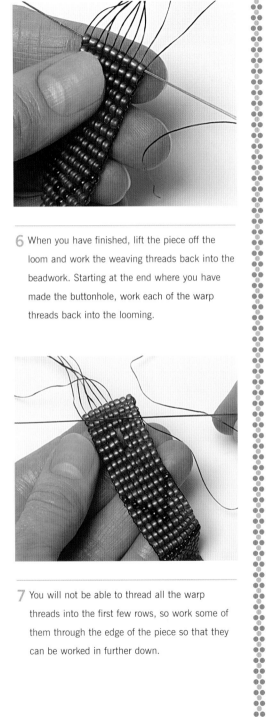

7 You will not be able to thread all the warp threads into the first few rows, so work some of them through the edge of the piece so that they can be worked in further down.

Adding a fastening bead or button

This is a slight variation on the method shown in Buttons and Loops (pages 90–91).

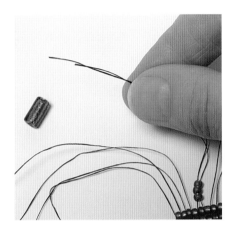

1 At the one end, choose the two central threads to attach your fastener to, and thread them through a few small beads.

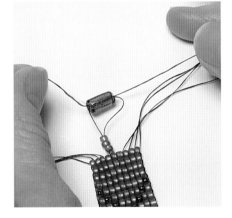

2 Divide the threads and work them into the fastener from either side, then back into the small beads.

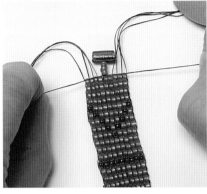

3 Knot these two threads together below the beads to strengthen the attachment, then work the rest of the warp threads back into the loomwork.

Using a bead as a fastener creates an attractive design feature.

LOOMING TIP

For a wider piece make several narrow strips and join them by weaving back through them off the loom.

Making a tab fastener

Rather than adding a button or bead to fasten your work, you can weave a tab on the loom to put through the buttonhole.

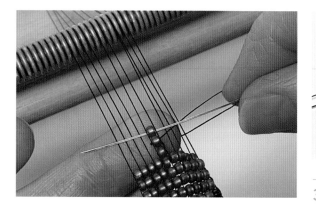

1 When your work has reached the required length, bring the thread up halfway through a row, then weave a few more rows on the loom, working a single bead on each row.

2 Work the weaving thread back down through these beads and back into the loomwork.

Work through the single row of beads to add more on either side.

3 Take the work off the loom and tidy the outside warp threads, leaving yourself one on either side of the single row of beads. Use these to add more beads on either side of the single row to create the tab.

4 Work these threads into the tab as many times as possible before finishing to make the tab as stiff as possible.

The finished tab fastener. Tension is important to create a flat tab.

Fringing and edge embellishment

Fringing is a great way to finish off a design.

There are a variety of different ways to enhance your loomwork by patterning the edges. These can be worked freehand, off the loom and as you are looming, and will contribute enormously to the versatility of your designs. As with other looming designs, they can be planned on a graph before you start work.

SINGLE-BEAD EDGING

This is done off the loom, with a fine beading needle.

Weave through a few rows to add a new thread.

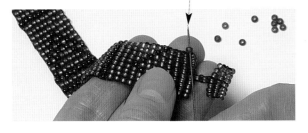

1 Take the work off the loom and tidy up all the threads. Add another thread to the work. Pick up a small bead and thread through the warp thread on the outside edge of the looming, and back through the bead.

You won't need to embellish the side that goes under a buttonhole.

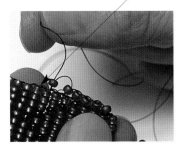

2 Put another bead onto the thread, work through the outside warp thread and back through the bead again. Continue in this way to create a neat edging band round the work.

TOOLS AND MATERIALS
- Fine or beading needles
- Synthetic thread

TRIPLE-BEAD EDGING

This can be worked in two different ways. You can either add the beads to the edges with a fine needle in the same way as for Single-Bead Edging (left), or run the needle back through the rows, adding additional beads at the ends of each one.

Working at the edges only

You work around the edges in this technique, using a fine beading needle.

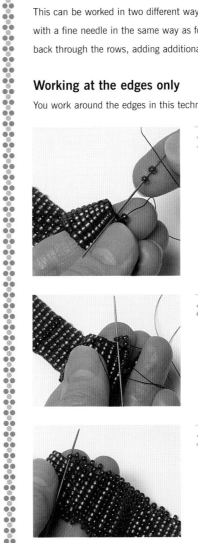

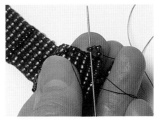

1 Take the work off the loom and tidy up all the threads. Attach another thread to the work and thread on one bead. Thread into the warp threads at the edge of the work, and back through the extra bead. Add two more beads and work back into the next loop between the rows.

2 Bring your needle back up into the second bead.

3 Continue in this way, picking up two beads, threading into the loop between the rows and back up into the closest bead.

Working through the rows

This is a way to add the edging if you are going to be backing or plaiting your warp threads and you won't need to run finishing threads into the rows. You can't use this method to embellish the ends of the work. It also stiffens the weaving. It can be worked off or on the loom.

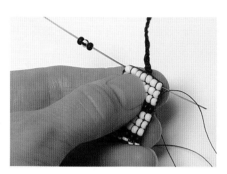

1 Attach another thread to the work, and using a long, fine beading needle work through the end row of the looming. Thread on three beads.

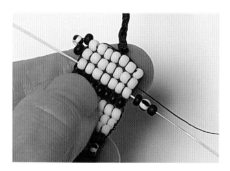

2 Work back into the next row, and add another three beads at the other side of the work. Continue in this way until both sides are finished.

FRINGING

Fringing can be added to your loomed work in different ways, either after the piece has been finished, or while you are looming.

Adding fringing

This can be done either on or off the loom, and at the same time as adding the triple-bead edge embellishment in Working through the rows (left).

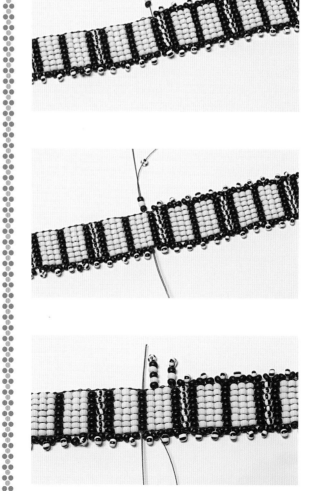

1 Attach another thread to the work in the position you wish the fringing to start. Work a beading needle through the row, adding more beads at one edge for the fringe. Start with a small amount of beads and bring the needle through them.

2 Work back into all but the last bead, which will hold the fringing in place.

3 Work back up the row for a close fringing. For a more spaced fringing, work back up the next row. Progress in this way, working up and down in either method.

Decorative loops

A variation on the off-loom fringing technique (left) is used to create loops below the loomwork.

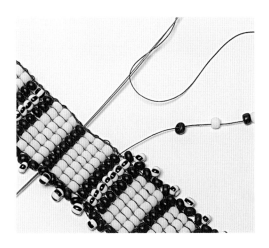

1 Attach another thread to the work in the position you wish the loops to start. Run the beading needle down the row and add on the extra beads. Work back up another row further along the work, leaving the additional beads hanging below.

2 This can be done in a simple or very intricate way, working into different rows and adding more loops of beads.

Integrated fringing

This is done on the loom as you work, but you still need to work through the rows twice.

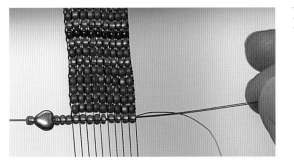

1 When you are ready to add the fringing, work down through a row again and add extra beads. You can work entirely in small beads or add other beads.

2 Thread back up all the beads except the bottom one, which will hold the fringe in place, and back into the row of beads on the loom.

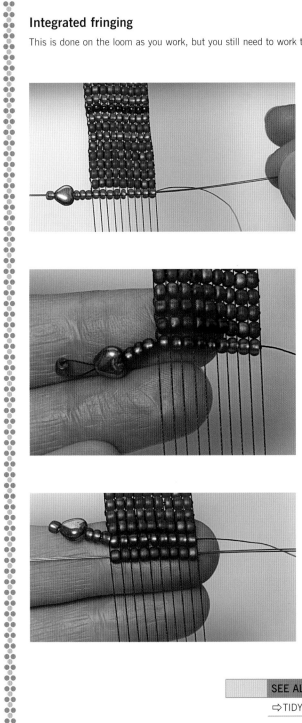

3 Add another row on the loom, then thread back down into it and add another fringe. Continue in this way until you have completed your fringing design.

SEE ALSO

⇨ TIDYING THE THREADS PAGE 89

BEADWEAVING

Beadweaving can be traced back to the ancient Egyptians and is enjoying a huge revival today, and in this section of the book we will be looking at the most popular off-loom techniques. With beadweaving it is the passage of the needle and thread that creates the stitches, and by using different sizes and shapes of beads, the look of the stitch can be altered.

A simple square stitch bracelet with graded colours.

Square stitch

You could be mistaken for thinking that a square stitch piece of beadwork has been worked on a loom. The two techniques are very similar in appearance, but the advantage of using square stitch is that you don't have all those ends to weave in, as you do for loomwork. Square stitch also serves as one of the most hard-wearing beading techniques because the thread travels through each bead several times. This stitch is also excellent for creating patterns because it works in a grid form. All that's needed is some graph paper, or alternatively, cross-stitch patterns transfer beautifully.

Getting the tension right

This is one of the easier stitches to work when it comes to keeping the tension right. Once you have been through the first two rows with your thread to straighten them, you can begin.

Single or double thread?

Only a single thread is required since the thread passes through each bead several times.

THE BASIC STITCH

Cylinder beads are often used with this stitch for two reasons. The first is that they are uniform and sit next to each other perfectly. Secondly, considering the size of bead, the central holes are fairly large, making it easier to accommodate the amount of thread that needs to pass through each bead. For this example size 11 cylinder beads were used.

BEADING TIP

It's a good idea to work through the steps creating samples which can be kept as a record to study later if necessary.

Stop bead.

1 Thread a long beading needle with 1.5m (1 ½ yards) of beading thread. Pick up a seed bead and slide it to within 15cm (6 inches) of the tail end of the thread. Bring the needle back up through the seed bead creating a loop around it. This is called the stop bead. Thread on nine more beads.

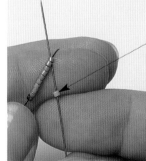

Beginners should start the second row with a different colour, making the newly added beads easier to see.

2 Pick up a bead and pass the thread back through the previous bead on the row.

INCREASING ON THE OUTSIDE EDGE

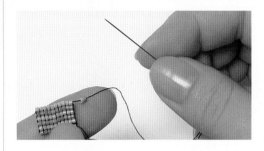

1 To increase on either of the outside edges, bring the needle through the last bead on the row you wish to increase. Thread on one more bead, plus the first bead of the next row.

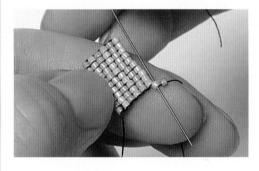

2 Thread back through the increase bead.

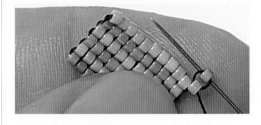

3 Thread through the first bead of the next row and continue along the row in the usual way. You can add as many beads as you wish for an increase, just square stitch your way back into the main section of the beadwork to secure.

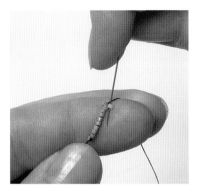

3 Turn the needle and pass the thread back through the bead you have just added.

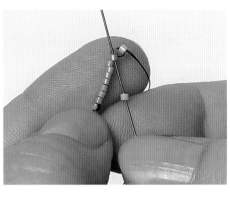

4 Pick up a bead and pass the needle back through the second from last bead of the first row.

5 Turn the needle and thread back through the bead just added. Continue adding individual beads and working along the row, threading through the adjacent bead of the previous row and back through the bead just added.

The needle passes through all the beads on the row each time.

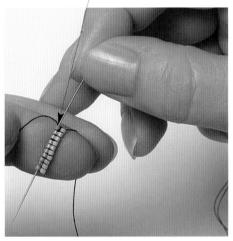

6 By the end of the row the beads may seem to be sitting slightly unevenly, so they need to be secured together. To do this, pass the needle back through the first row of beads, then turn and come back through the second row. Follow Steps 2–6 to add more rows of beads.

DECREASING ON THE OUTSIDE EDGE

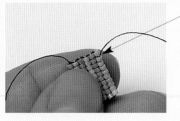

The next row is started here, one bead in from the outside edge.

1 Work square stitch in the normal way until you finish the row before the one you wish to make the decrease on. Thread back as usual through the previous row, then begin to thread through the row just added. Bring the needle out at the place you wish the decrease to begin.

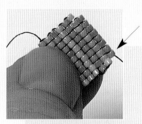

The decrease can now be seen.

2 Thread on a bead and go back through the bead the thread is coming out of, then back through the bead just added. Continue along the row until you reach the bead where you wish to stop the row.

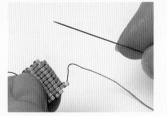

3 Add the first bead of the next row and continue as usual.

TUBULAR SQUARE STITCH

Tubular square stitch is best worked over an existing cylinder, such as a drinking straw, plastic tube or pen. It can be used to make rope necklaces, vessels and tubes.

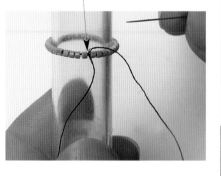

Use a double knot to secure the beads.

1 Thread on as many beads as necessary to fit around your chosen tubular form. Wrap the threaded beads around the cylinder and double knot into place.

Working counterclockwise for Row 2.

3 Thread back through the first bead, then through the bead just added. You will notice that you are working counterclockwise. Work in the same way as flat square stitch to complete the row.

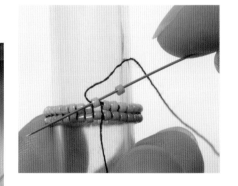

2 Thread through the first bead along and pick up the first bead of the next row.

4 When the second row is complete, take the thread back through the row you have just completed, then bring the needle out through the first bead added in Row 2, ready to begin Row 3, which will be worked clockwise round.

Brick stitch

Brick stitch, also known as *Comanche* stitch, after the Native American peoples, is a much more solid stitch than many of the other widely used techniques. If you look at a flat piece of brick stitch, you will see that it resembles a brick wall, hence the name.

Brick stitch is widely used in its tubular form to create amulet purses and, since it is a fairly firm stitch, it can also be used to create freestanding beadwork such as vessels and three-dimensional pieces.

When working brick stitch you may wish to incorporate a pattern within the piece. If so, you will find that cylinder beads and brick stitch sit perfectly together, due to the uniformity of the beads and the regularity of the stitch, making them a great combination.

A brick stitch bracelet worked in cubes to great effect.

Single or double thread?

Brick stitch is generally worked with a single thread. This is because the technique requires the thread to be passed through the same bead twice. If double thread were used the bead – especially if a bugle bead – could become "clogged" with thread, at which point the needle would be difficult to pull through, and, if forced, the bead may shatter.

Getting the tension right

When working brick stitch be careful not to pull too tightly, since the beadwork will over tighten and a "wavy" effect will be produced.

STARTING THE LADDER

This first step forms the foundation row for brick stitch. It can be worked with either bugle or seed beads, depending on your choice of project. Many amulet purses have a bugle ladder top, and using bugles is quite a good way to familiarize yourself with the stitch since they are not quite as fiddly as seed beads.

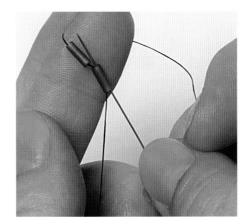

1 Thread a long beading needle with 1.5m (1 ½ yards) of beading thread. Pick up a seed bead and slide it to within 15cm (6 inches) of the tail end of the thread. Bring the needle back up through the seed bead creating a loop around it. This is called the stop bead. Thread on nine more beads.

BEADING TIP

Every now and then you will come across a badly cut or chipped bugle bead. Discard it immediately, otherwise it will cut your thread and the beadwork will simply fall apart. The more you pay for bugle beads, the better the quality.

2 Pull both the tail end and the needle end of the thread in opposite directions. This will make the bugles "click" together, sitting snugly side by side.

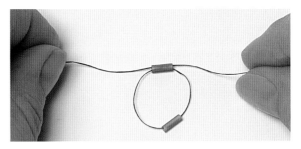

The tail end sits on the left-hand side of the beadwork.

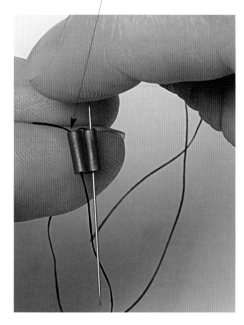

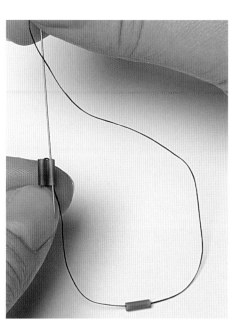

The needle is threaded back up through the third bugle in order to be in the correct position to add the next bugle.

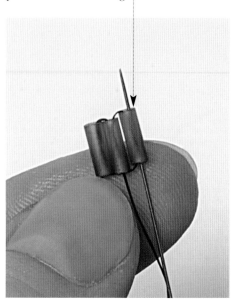

3 Hold the beads between your thumb and forefinger with the tail end sitting to the left-hand side. Take the needle back down through the second bugle, from top to bottom.

4 Thread on a third bugle and take the needle back through the second bugle, from top to bottom.

5 Pull the thread through and down towards the tail end until the third bugle sits against the second bugle. Thread back up through the third bugle.

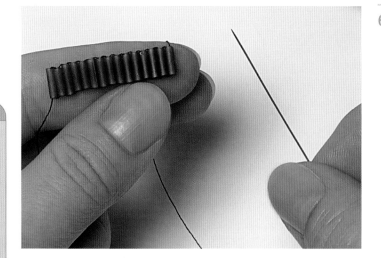

BEADING TIP

To keep the tension firm always pull the working thread back towards you and the tail end of the thread. If you pull the thread away from your beadwork the tension will slacken and you will begin to see daylight between the bugle beads.

6 Continue adding bugles in the same manner until the foundation row reaches the required length. Notice that you are alternating between taking the needle through the top and bottom of the previous bugle added. Remember not to thread your needle through the side of the bead your working thread is protruding from.

ADDING ROWS OF SEED BEADS

Once the foundation row of bugle beads is in place, rows of brick stitch can be added.

The needle passes down through the bead and the loop.

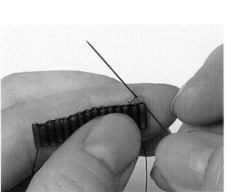

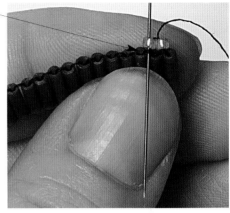

1 To add the first row of brick stitch, thread on two seed beads. Take the needle through the second loop of the bugle ladder from back to front, letting the two seed beads sit side by side with holes pointing upwards.

2 Take the needle back up through the first seed bead.

3 Now take the needle down through the second seed bead, and through the loop of the bugle ladder once more.

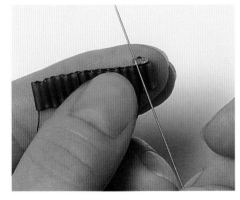

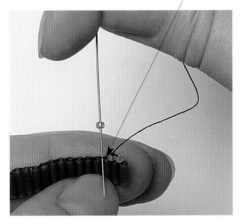

When the bead is picked up the needle passes through the loop.

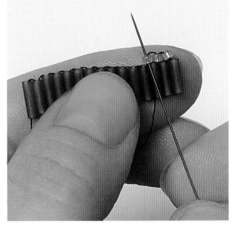

4 Turn the needle and travel back up through the second bead. These moves at the beginning of each row will help anchor the first bead and stop it tipping inwards, giving a flat, even piece of beadwork. This movement is known as the "locking" stitch.

5 Pick up a third seed bead and take the needle through the next loop along the bugle row.

6 Pull the thread through the loop until the bead sits nicely next to the previous beads. Thread the needle back up through the bead and gently pull upwards until all three beads sit nicely in a row. Continue in the same manner, one bead at a time along the row.

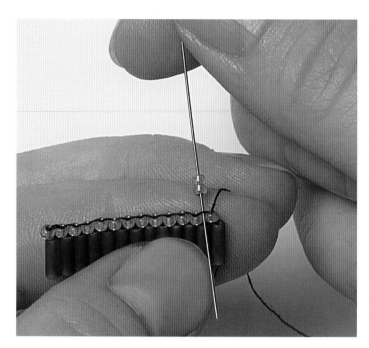

7 To begin Row 2, turn the stitching over and pick up two seed beads. Thread the needle through the last loop of the first row of seed beads, letting the new two seed beads sit side by side with holes pointing upwards.

CHANGING THREAD

In the case of the bugle ladder, you can simply thread back through three or four beads then double knot using the next loop along, remembering to take the needle through two or three more beads once knotted.

To start a new thread, thread up and down through the beads, roughly six to seven beads back from your start point, double knot and thread through until you reach the section you need to continue.

8 Thread back up through the first bead, then down through the second bead and the first loop once again, then back up through the second bead. Continue adding one bead at a time as before until you finish the row.

9 Add subsequent rows until the beadwork reaches the required length.

INCREASING ON THE OUTSIDE EDGE

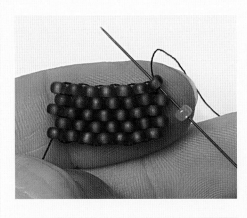

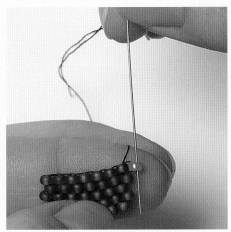

The increase of two beads in position with the next row added on top.

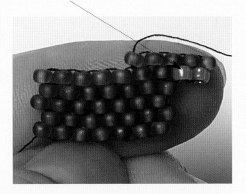

1 When you reach the point where you require an increase, thread on one seed bead, then pass back up through the seed bead the thread is coming out of.

2 Take the needle back down through the seed bead you have just added.

3 Add as many beads in this same way as you need, then continue to brick stitch the next row, including the increase beads.

DECREASING ON THE OUTSIDE EDGE

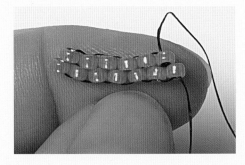

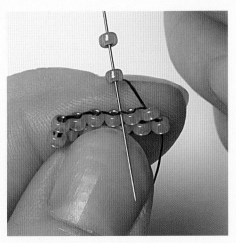

1 To begin the row you wish to decrease, thread on two beads, only this time thread through the second loop in from the end of the previous row. Take the needle back up through the first bead, then down through the second bead, the same loop, then back up through the second bead once more. Continue along the row adding one bead at a time as before.

2 To begin the next row, pick up two beads. Thread through the second loop in from the end of the previous row.

3 As you add further rows the beadwork will naturally decrease down to a point. You can then thread back down through the beadwork to one of the outside beads on the initial row and complete the other side in exactly the same way, creating a diamond shape.

TUBULAR BRICK STITCH

Once the foundation row is in place, tubular brick stitch is a firm and satisfying stitch to work.

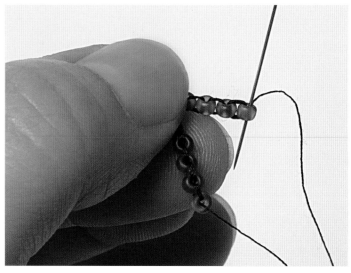

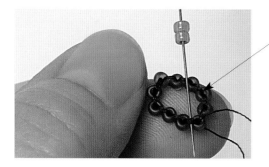

1 Work the foundation row following the instructions for Starting the Ladder on page 101, only this time using as many seed beads as necessary to make the tube to the required width. To make the base more stable you can thread through the beads from one end back to your finishing point.

2 Lay the ladder on a flat surface with the bead holes facing upwards. Take the needle down through the first bead of the ladder, then back up through the last bead. Go back through both beads again to secure the circle.

Make sure that all the holes are facing upwards.

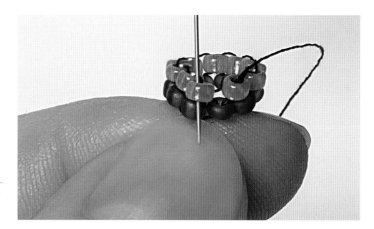

3 Make sure the working thread is coming out of a bead on the opposite side of the circle to the tail end thread. Start a new row by threading on two beads. Pass the needle through the next loop along, then back up through the first bead, down through the second bead, and loop as before. Bring it back up through the second bead once more. Continue adding one bead at a time for the remainder of the row.

4 When you arrive back at the beginning of the row, thread the needle back down through the first bead of the row, then back up through the last bead. You are now ready to start the next row, remembering always the two-bead start.

Herringbone stitch

Herringbone stitch has endless possibilities, as you will see while working through the various samples. Increasing and decreasing can create some wonderful shapes and textures with this stitch, so try experimenting with different shaped beads and you'll make some great discoveries.

Single or double thread?

As a general guide, one strand of thread should suit most beading. However, if you require a firm tension, perhaps for a three-dimensional piece, a double length of thread helps tighten the tension.

Getting the tension right

It is certainly true to say that the more you practise this stitch, the better your tension will become. Too loose and the beads will flop about, making it difficult to see where to make your next move. Too tight and the beads will buckle up, and you won't get that fantastic chevron look. Over time you will perfect the tension that suits you.

Tubular herringbone worked with triangle beads gives a great textural effect.

LADDER STITCH STARTING METHOD

There are two ways in which to start herringbone stitch. The first is from a ladder stitch base, making it slightly easier to start since the ladder forms quite a firm base. This method of starting is recommended for those new to herringbone stitch. Size 8 seed beads in two colours have been used in the following steps so that the thread and bead patterns can be easily identified when working.

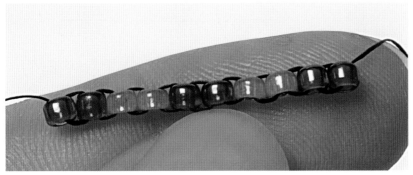

1 Make a ladder foundation row following the instructions for Starting the Ladder on page 101, only this time using size 8 seed beads in pairs of two colours. Eight beads will make a good-sized practice piece.

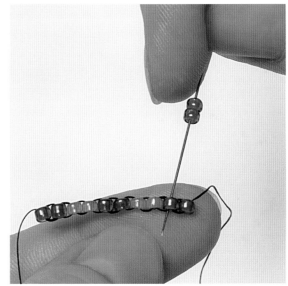

2 To form Row 2, pick up a pair of seed beads in the first colour, to match the pair at the end of the initial row. Take the needle down through the second bead along on the foundation row and gently pat the two new beads so that they sit side by side with the holes facing upwards.

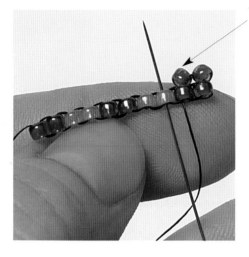

Make sure that the beads sit above the first "pairs" of beads. The holes of the beads should be facing upwards.

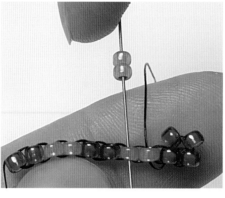

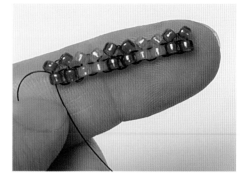

3 Bring the needle up through the third bead in the ladder row.

4 Thread on the next pair of beads in the alternative colour and take the needle down through the fourth bead along the foundation row. Gently pat the new pair of beads until they sit side by side with holes facing upwards. Work the rest of the row in the same way.

5 As you complete the second row you will notice the herringbone or chevron effect starting to appear, with each pair of beads slightly tilting toward each other. At this point the beads are sitting in matching pairs, but it is the next row that connects the pairs together.

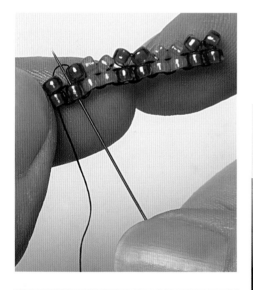

The thread moves in a diagonal direction. Ensure the needle is in the correct position to begin Row 3.

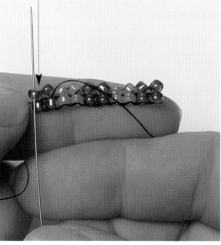

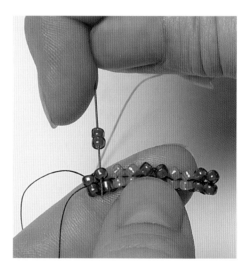

6 The thread is trailing from the first bead of the original ladder row. We now need to make a couple of moves to ensure that the working thread is coming out of the left-hand bead of the first set of pairs. Take the needle up through the second bead along on the original ladder.

7 Now take it across and up through the left-hand bead of the first pair on Row 2.

8 Now for Row 3. Thread on a pair of beads to match those directly below. Pass the needle down through the second bead of the first pair of Row 2.

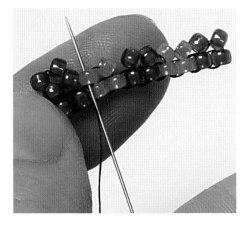

9 Come up through the first bead of the next pair along on Row 2. This creates the "linking" stitch between each pair of beads.

The diagonal move is repeated to enable Row 4 to begin.

The linking stitch that connects the pairs together.

10 Thread on two beads in the second colour and bring the needle down through the right-hand bead of the pair below, on Row 2.

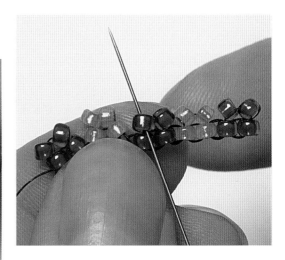

11 Take the needle up through the first bead of the next pair along on Row 2 and continue along the row in the same manner.

13 Continue building up rows in the same way.

BEADING TIP

Remember, when linking the pairs together you are only threading up and down through the row you are working on, not two or three rows below it.

12 You will notice from the finished row that the thread is not in the correct place for starting the next row. Take the needle back up through the next bead on Row 2, then through the right-hand bead of the first pair on Row 3. You are now ready to begin Row 4.

THREE-ROW STARTING METHOD

The second starting method incorporates all of the first three rows at once. This gives a more equally spaced look from the start. However, when you first attempt this method, you may find it quite difficult to get the tension right, but persevere, since it gives a great result. Using three different coloured size 8 seed beads helps tremendously with this technique.

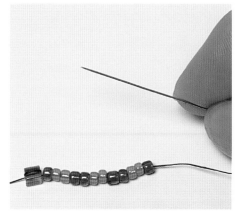

1 Thread a long beading needle with 1m (1 yard) of beading thread. Pick up a bead and slide it to within 15cm (6 inches) of the tail end of the thread. Bring the needle back up through the seed beads, creating a loop around it to form the stop bead (this will be removed when the beadwork is complete). Thread a row of 12 seed beads, consisting of a single red bead followed by pairs of alternating orange and red beads, and finishing with a single red bead – or, of course, colours of your choosing.

The thread is passed over the first pair of orange beads.

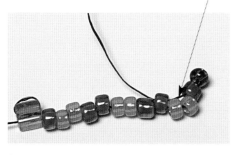

2 Thread on one topaz bead. Pass the needle back through the last bead added on the original row, then through the first bead of the next pair of red beads.

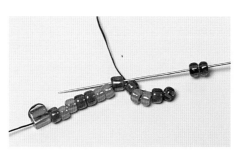

3 Thread on two topaz beads and pass the needle through the second red bead of that pair.

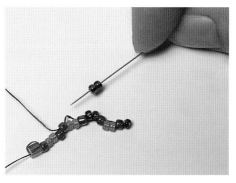

4 Take the needle through the first bead of the next pair of red beads and add on two more topaz beads.

BEADING TIP

At the end of each row you are applying both the last bead of the row you are working on and the first bead of the next row.

5 Pass the needle through the second red bead of that pair and repeat as before.

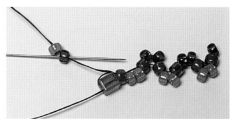

6 When you reach the end of the row, pass the needle through the single red bead. Thread on one topaz and one orange bead. Thread back down through the topaz bead only.

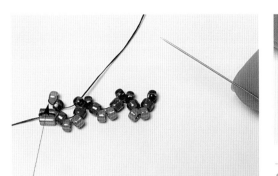

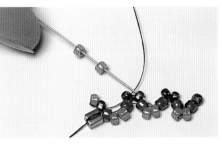

The orange bead becomes the first bead of the next row now being added.

7 Pass the needle up through the first topaz bead of the next pair along. Thread on two orange beads.

8 Thread through the second bead of the pair of topaz beads and continue along the row as before.

9 When you have threaded through the very last single topaz bead of the row, you then add one orange and one red bead. Go back through the orange bead, bypassing the red bead, then finally through the first orange bead of the next pair along.

10 Continue working in the same way to build up several rows.

Herringbone stitch looks wonderful when worked with different shapes and textures of beads. In this example 4mm cubes have been used to interesting effect.

INCREASING BETWEEN COLUMNS

When working herringbone stitch, increasing can be done between columns of pairs or between the pairs themselves.

The orange beads show increasing very clearly.

Work herringbone stitch in the usual way until you reach the point at which you require an increase. As you move from one pair of beads to the other, add a bead onto the loop before you come up through the first bead of the next pair. This adds an increase of one bead. Always start with one bead, then you can build up to two beads on the outside columns only, to give a gentle increase.

BEADING TIP

After the initial row you can start to pull up on the beadwork, making it fall into an even herringbone.

INCREASING BETWEEN PAIRS

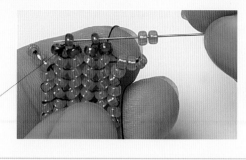

Three beads are added where two would normally sit.

At the increase point, add three beads within the pair instead of the usual two. On the return row, add two beads to each side of the three bead increases creating two extra columns.

DECREASING BETWEEN COLUMNS

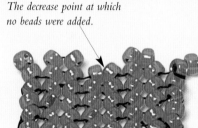

The decrease point at which no beads were added.

1 Decreasing between columns is a quick way to decrease. At the required decreasing point, thread through the next pair along without adding any beads, then continue along the row as normal.

2 For the next row, skip that same pair altogether, this time pulling on the thread to close the gap.

DECREASING BETWEEN PAIRS

Adding three beads between two pairs gives a gentle and even increase.

1 At the decrease point bring the needle up through the first bead in a pair. Thread on three beads, then take the needle down through the second bead of the next column along.

2 On the return journey, bring the needle up through the first of the three added beads. Thread on two beads of the next row and come down through the third of the three added beads. Continue along the row.

3 Treat the new pair of beads as a new column and continue to herringbone along the row.

CIRCULAR HERRINGBONE STITCH

This technique forms a flat circle of beads useful for the base of a vessel or cylinder.

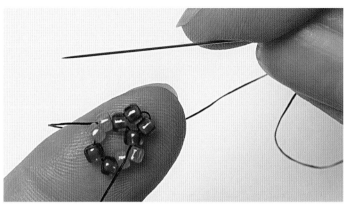

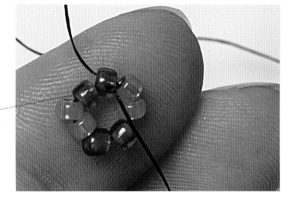

The double knot secures the circle but it shouldn't be tied too tightly.

1 Thread on eight size 8 seed beads in alternating pairs of two colours. Tie the thread into a circle using a double knot between the first and last bead. Take the needle through the first bead of the next pair along.

2 Thread on two beads to match the colour of the bead you have just passed the needle through. Pass through the second bead of the initial pair, then thread through to the first bead of the next pair along.

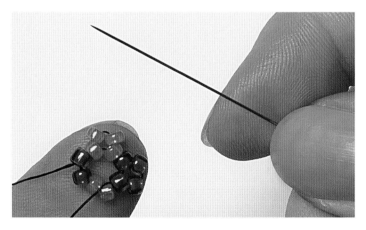

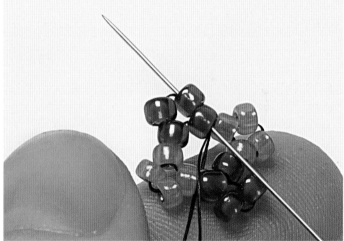

3 Thread on two beads to match this second colour, then through the second bead of the pair and through the first bead of the next pair along.

4 When you have come full circle, it is time to step up. Thread through the first beads of the first pairs of Rows 1 and 2. You will see that quite a large gap has opened up between the columns. Fill these with increase beads when threading from one group of pairs to the next to create a stunning pattern. Of course you can add more "spokes" at the start of your beadwork by adding more pairs of beads in the initial circle. You could also use size 11 seed beads, which would make it more delicate and smaller in size.

TUBULAR HERRINGBONE STITCH

This stitch makes a great tube, suitable for a
necklace or bracelet. Try working this technique
with size 5 triangle beads in two contrasting
colours. Although the tension takes a little
mastering, it's well worth it.

2 Thread on two triangles in a contrasting colour.
Take the needle down through the next bead
along on the initial row, then up through the third
triangle along. Repeat, adding two more pairs
of beads.

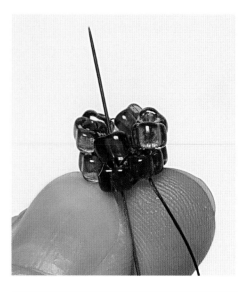

3 To step up, thread back up through the first
triangle on the initial row, then through the first
bead of the first pair on the second row. You are
now ready to start Row 3.

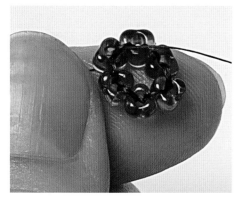

1 Make a ladder foundation row following the
instructions for Ladder Stitch Starting Method on
page 107, only this time using six size 5 triangle
beads. Form a circle with the holes of the beads
pointing upwards, then join together by threading
through the first and last triangles on the ladder
several times.

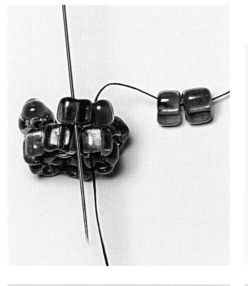

4 Pick up two beads and pass down through the
left-hand bead of the second row.

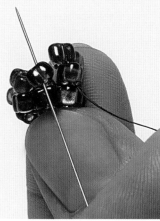

5 Bring the needle up through the first bead of the
next pair along. This is your linking stitch.
Continue adding rows until you reach the
required length.

BEADING TIP

Start to hold the tube between your
thumb and forefinger as soon as
you can to encourage the beadwork
upwards. Always pull upwards on
the thread when working.

Netting stitch

Although netting stitch became particularly popular in Victorian times, it actually dates back to ancient Egypt. This stitch produces a very open, lacy effect, and because of this drapes beautifully around the neck and wrist. It can also be worked firmly enough to make a tube. This stitch may be slightly more limiting than the others, but it is still very impressive.

A simple yet effective netted choker.

Single or double thread?

One strand of beading thread is perfect for this technique. However, if you wish to experiment with freestanding or three-dimensional beadwork, two strands will give a firmer base, but look out for knots.

Getting the tension right

It is a good idea to work this stitch flat on a bead mat; that way you can see when the tension needs altering. Too loose and the thread will show, too tight and the netting will buckle. Another tip is to try not to pierce the working thread that is already sitting in the bead, since this will result in the netting twisting and not laying completely flat.

FIVE-BEAD NETTING STITCH

This technique forms the basis of all netting stitches: it's just the number of beads used that varies. For this example we have used size 11 seed beads in red and black, but of course you can use two colours of your choosing.

1 Thread a long beading needle with 1m (1 yard) of beading thread. Thread on one black seed bead and slide it to within 15cm (6 inches) of the tail end of the thread. Bring the needle back up through the seed bead, creating a loop around it to secure it as the stop bead. Pick up two red, one black and two red beads until you have 24 beads in total, including the stop bead.

2 Bring the needle back up through the 12th bead (black), from the bottom. Pull up to form the first diamond. There should be a black bead at all four points of the diamond.

BEADING TIP

To ensure that the beadwork sits evenly when working netting stitch do not pull the thread too tightly.

The needle moves through the sixth bead.

3 Pick up two red, one black and two red beads. Count up five beads on the original row and thread up through the sixth (black) bead.

There is a black bead at the corner of each diamond and the needle passes through one of them.

5 Pick up two red, one black and two red beads again. Take the needle down through the middle black bead of the last diamond of the previous row.

The central side bead of the diamond about to be formed.

7 Pick up two red, one black, two red, one black and two red beads. Thread back up through the middle black bead of the last diamond of the previous row.

4 Make one more diamond in exactly the same way as in Step 3, finishing the row by taking the needle up through the stop bead.

6 Pick up two red, one black and two red beads. Take the needle down through the second middle black bead of the previous row – forming another diamond. Repeat to make one more diamond.

8 As you progress, you will start to see the netting pattern emerge. Continue adding rows until the netting is the required length.

INCREASING

To increase, simply place more beads on the thread when forming the diamond loops. Here the increase loops have been added in black. Alternatively, you can add more intersection beads, perhaps two beads to a loop.

Netting stitch is enlarged quickly with the use of increase loops.

DECREASING

To decrease, all you need to do is add three beads to a diamond loop instead of the initial five beads.

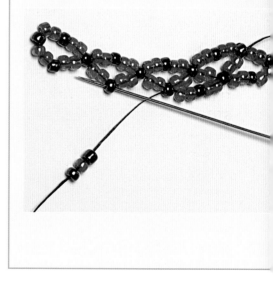

CIRCULAR NETTING STITCH

This technique produces a flat disc of stitching that is often used for encasing Christmas baubles. You increase slightly as you work each row.

Take the needle through the third black bead.

Repeat three times.

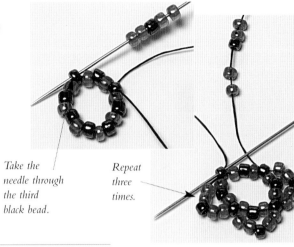

1 Thread on 16 beads, red and black alternately. Take the needle back through the beads to form a circle. Thread through the first black bead once again.

2 Pick up two red, one black and two red beads. Skipping the second black bead on the original circle, take the needle through the third black bead. Repeat three times.

3 At the first black bead, take the needle through. Thread back down the first loop, bringing the needle out of the middle (black) bead. Pick up three red, one black and three red beads. Take the needle through the black bead of the next loop.

TUBULAR NETTING STITCH

Tubular netting makes for an interesting necklace and bracelet, and you can also work one netted tube over another to produce an impressive effect. It is quite useful to work this stitch over a drinking straw; this helps with the tension which should be kept constant throughout.

The needle passes through the second black bead.

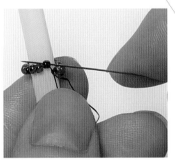

1 Pick up one black and two red beads until you have 15 beads in total. Wrap the beads around a drinking straw and tie in a double knot. Take the needle through the first black bead once again.

2 Pick up two red, one black and two red beads (remembering to skip the first black bead along), then take the needle through the second black bead as worked in flat circular netting.

3 You will notice after forming the second loop that as you go to attach the third loop there is only one black bead left. Since the stitch is spiralling, you need to go through the black bead of the first loop added on this row. This effectively is your step up. Continue to add rows until the desired length is reached.

Peyote stitch

Peyote stitch is one of the most versatile and best-loved off-loom beadwork techniques used in the world today. It is a very flexible stitch, and when worked it almost feels like a fabric.

Thread tension plays a large part in the final appearance and texture of this stitch. The stop bead not only plays a vital role in keeping the first row of beads from falling off the tail end of your thread, but also allows you to tighten the tension of the beadwork.

Two peyote-stitched purse pendants.

Single or double thread?

Peyote stitch is usually worked with a single thread. If you wish the project to be freestanding, you could consider a double or thicker thread, but this does tend to knot and tangle more easily. Work several samples to see what suits you best.

Getting the tension right

The first two or three rows of peyote stitch can seem difficult to control. You should work the stitch in your hands and avoid trying to bead on the table, because at some point you will have to pick your work up. The first row is best held between your thumb and forefinger with the tail end of the thread wrapped around your little finger. To tighten the tension pull the thread firmly in the direction you are working in and push the stop bead up towards the main beadwork.

When working tubular peyote stitch, the tension has to be firm from the start, particularly when the beadwork is required to stand without support.

EVEN-COUNT PEYOTE STITCH

For beginners, peyote stitch is easier to achieve with an even number of beads. An odd count involves manoeuvring the needle and thread through several beads to arrive in the right place and direction to start the next row, so should only be attempted once you have mastered the even-count method. The samples shown here have been worked using size 8 seed beads in two colours to ensure the sequence is easy to follow.

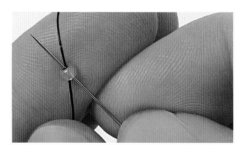

1 Thread a long beading needle with 1m (1 yard) of beading thread. Pick up a seed bead and slide it to within 15cm (6 inches) of the tail end of the thread. Bring the needle back up through the seed bead creating a loop around the bead to secure it as the stop bead. Thread on seven more seed beads of the same colour.

Hold the initial beads between your thumb and forefinger.

Pass the needle through the next bead along.

2 Pick up another seed bead in a second colour. Let it rest next to the last bead on the first row, then take the needle through the next bead along on the first row. This will bring the newly added bead on top of the first bead of the initial row to begin forming the second row. Thread on another bead, and missing out the adjacent bead of the first row, pass the needle through the next bead in the row. Add four beads in total.

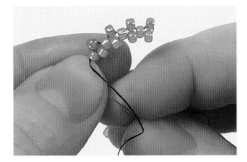

*Take the
needle
through
the next
bead along.*

*The bead sits
on top of the
first bead of the
previous row.*

3 Look at the row you've just completed – you can see the gaps between the beads. This is where you need to place the beads for the next row. If at the end of the second row you notice the tension is a little loose and the beads are not sitting correctly, place your thumbnail against the stop bead and push it up towards the other beads.

4 Pick up another bead in the first colour and let it rest on top of the stop bead. Take the needle through the next bead along, which is sitting slightly above the initial row of beads. Continue in the same way to the end of the row.

5 At this point you may find it easier to flip your beadwork over. Pick up a bead, let it sit on top of the first bead of the row beneath. Take the needle through the next bead along sitting slightly above. Continue along to the end of the row. Keep adding more rows until you are confident about working the stitch.

TWO-NEEDLE START

If you find starting peyote stitch a little difficult, you can always try starting with two needles.

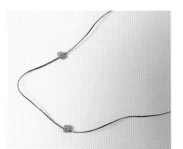

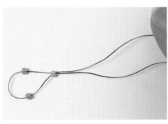

1 Cut 1.5m (1 ½ yards) of beading thread and thread a beading needle onto both ends of the same thread. Pick up two seed beads, taking them down towards the middle of the looped thread.

2 Thread a seed bead onto one of the needles, then pass the other needle through the same bead. Push the bead down towards the first two beads. This will make the first two beads sit one above the other, with the last bead alongside both.

3 Pick up one new bead with each needle. Push the beads down towards the first three beads. The pattern is now beginning to resemble peyote stitch. Continue in the same manner until you have the length of base you require. To start the next row, revert to one needle and thread; the other can be left to one side until your working thread runs out and needs to be replaced.

CHANGING THREAD

Attach your new working thread before you finish off the old thread. Bring the newly threaded needle up six to eight beads diagonally back from the bead that the working thread emerges from. Thread the needle through the first three beads, leaving a tail of about 10cm (4 inches). Double knot the new thread between the next two beads along, then bring the needle through the last two or three beads (including the bead the old working thread is coming out of) and tug gently. Rethread the initial working thread. Take it diagonally down through a few beads in the opposite direction and double knot. Take the thread through two or three more beads and then cut off.

ODD-COUNT PEYOTE STITCH

Odd-count peyote stitch is used when a centre point is required in the pattern of your design. You will notice that a little juggling is required when starting a new row on the edge of the beadwork.

This bead will sit on top of the stop bead on the initial row.

1 Using a stop bead as with Even-Count Peyote Stitch, page 118, thread on nine beads. Peyote stitch along the row until you reach the first and second beads of the initial row. Pass the needle through both beads, keeping a firm tension. Pick up a bead, which will be the last bead of the third row, and pass the needle through the second bead in from the first. Pass the needle through the lower bead of the next pair along.

BEADING TIP

When first attempting peyote stitch you may choose to work with cylinder beads. Their straight edges let them sit well next to each other, making the stitch pattern easier to see. However, when moving onto freeform work, you will find the roundness of the seed bead will mould, shape and gel together much more easily.

2 Turn the needle and pass it through the top bead of the pair, with the needle facing back towards the stop-bead end of the row.

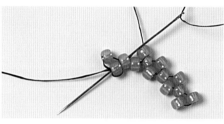

3 Thread back through the next single bead along and then through the stop bead.

The thread has gone through the next single bead and the stop bead.

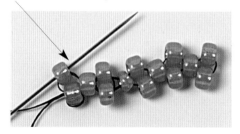

4 Turn the needle and thread back up through the last bead of Row 3 once more. You are now ready to start the next row. As you progress, you will notice that you only have to take your thread on this long adventure on one edge of the beadwork; the other edge will turn as for even-count peyote.

INCREASING MID ROW

Mid-row increases blend into the beadwork extremely well, and since peyote is such a flexible stitch, it's great for covering objects, forms and moulds.

1 Work peyote stitch as normal until an increase is required. Pick up two beads instead of one and place them in exactly the same way as you would if using a single bead.

2 When returning on the next row, take the thread through the first bead of the pair added. Thread on another bead, then take the needle through the second bead of the pair and continue along to the end of the row. Alternatively, you can place two beads above the first increase on the previous row, so that these beads are effectively treated as one. You can increase as many times as you wish.

DECREASING MID ROW

As with mid-row increasing, peyote stitch can be very smoothly decreased mid row. Being able to increase and decrease so easily, combined with the use of different tensions, makes this stitch a joy to work three-dimensional projects with.

Stitch along the row as normal until you reach the point where you wish to decrease, then simply take the needle across the gap, without adding a bead, and thread into the next bead along. Pull up firmly to close the gap. On the next row, when you reach the decrease, place one bead over the gap where the decrease occurred, then pull up tightly. You can decrease as many times as you wish within any one row; it all depends on how rapidly you need to do it.

TWO-DROP PEYOTE STITCH

This is a fast way of working peyote stitch, but you can also achieve some interesting textured beadwork with it. It's also possible to work a three-, even four-drop peyote, and it's worth experimenting with this technique, which also works in the tubular form of the stitch. It's a good idea to use two different coloured beads to start with, making the stitch easier to follow.

1 Thread on one seed bead and take the needle back through the bead to anchor it as the stop bead. Starting with one bead the same colour as the stop bead, thread on nine more beads to create five pairs of matching colours.

2 Pick up two beads in the same colour as the last two of the first row. Let them lie directly above the last pair, then take the needle through the next two beads along. Continue along the row in the same manner.

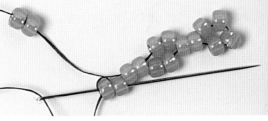

3 To start the next row, thread through the first pair of seed beads once more, then add the first pair of the next row.

THREE-DROP PEYOTE STITCH

Try experimenting by using other sizes of beads to add texture and interest to your beadwork.

Three-drop peyote stitch is worked in exactly the same way as two drop, only this time working in threes. Within this piece of beadwork, 6mm bugle beads have been added so that it almost becomes controlled "freeform".

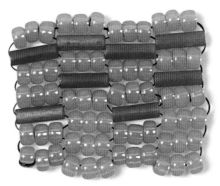

CIRCULAR PEYOTE STITCH

This variation of peyote stitch produces a flat circular piece of beadwork, great for making lids or covering the bottom of vessels. Use two different colours of seed beads when you first practise this technique to highlight each new row and allow you to follow the pattern of the beads more easily.

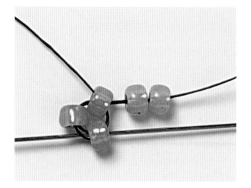

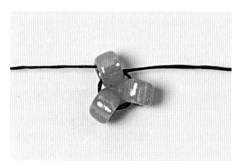

1 Thread on three seed beads and push them down to within 15cm (6 inches) of the tail end of the thread. Pass the needle through the three beads once more to form a circle.

2 To start Row 2, add two seed beads between each bead of the first row. Step up by threading the needle through the first bead on the previous row, then through the first bead of the first pair added on this row.

3 On Row 3, add a seed bead between each bead of the previous row; this includes adding a bead between each pair from the last row. To step up, thread back through the first bead added on the last row, then through the first bead added on this row.

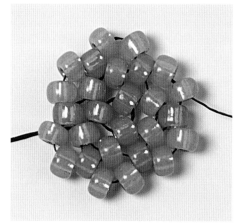

4 On Row 4 add two beads between each bead from the previous row. Step up by threading up through the first bead from the previous row, then through the first pair added on this row.

5 On Row 5 add one bead in between each bead from the previous row, including pairs. To step up, thread through the first bead from the previous row, then the last bead on this row. Keep adding subsequent rows until your beadwork is the required size. Sometimes you will need to add two beads, other times only one bead will need to be used.

BEADING TIP

If you increase too much at one time, your work will start to frill, so use your eye to judge the number of beads required. However, you may wish to encourage frilling since this can produce wonderfully organic shapes and textures.

TUBULAR PEYOTE

Tubular peyote creates a hollow tube, and it can be worked around any cylindrical object, such as a drinking straw or some dowelling. A clear drinking straw is a good choice when you first attempt the stitch, since it allows you to see your work clearly. This technique has been used widely for beaded needle cases and pictorial amulet purses.

When working this stitch, you can start off with an odd or even number of beads. If using an even number, you will need to step up at the end of each row. This is the best method when creating a pattern or pictorial piece. If using an odd number, you will just spiral up to the next row.

The following example shows even-count working. Just think of it as exactly the same as flat even-count peyote, only worked in a tube!

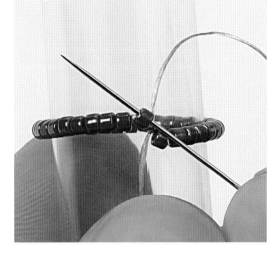

1 Thread on an even number of beads and tie in a double knot around a tubular object, leaving a tiny gap between the first and last bead in the circle. (Don't overlap the beads or the stitch will not lie correctly and be impossible to work.) Take the needle back through the first bead once more.

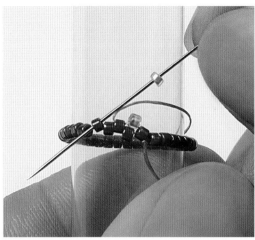

2 Pick up one bead and let it sit above the next bead along. Then take the needle through the third bead along from the start of the initial row of beads. Pull slightly as you take the thread through the bead; this will make the two beads sit nicely one on top of the other. Continue along the row in this way until you arrive back at the first bead added.

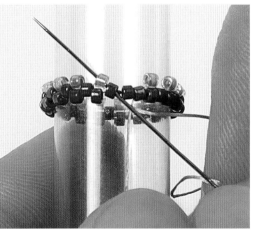

3 To step up, take the needle through both the first bead of the initial row and the first bead of this row to move up to the next row to be added. Continue to add rows in the same way until you achieve the required length of tube.

BEADING TIP

This technique is especially effective when worked with cylinder beads, since they sit so neatly together, especially when creating a picture. However, seed beads will give added texture to the work. Try using both types of beads to see the different effects for yourself.

Right-angle weave

Right-angle weave is one of the most versatile and fluid stitches found among the beadweaving techniques. This makes it a very useful stitch for covering odd shapes: increasing and decreasing instantly alters the beadwork to fit over almost any shape. The stitch is so called because the beads sit at right angles to each other. Worked in groups of four beads that link together to form a chain effect, the thread travels a certain path, round and round in opposite circles to give the beadwork great flexibility and texture. If the path of the thread is not followed properly the beadwork will become rigid, losing its fabric-like appeal.

This stitch can also be worked using groups of three beads on each of the four sides, which gives a square effect to each link. This is often referred to as square netting.

Amulet bag stitched in right-angle weave, embellished with cubes and seed beads.

Size 8 beads have been used to demonstrate the workings of the stitch. When you are confident with the technique you can try using size 11 seed beads for a great effect.

Choosing a thread

Due to the complex path of the thread, the beads are passed through several times, so a single thread is best to prevent the beads from becoming clogged.

Getting the tension right

Right-angle weave can seem quite tricky to hold at the start, but once you have the first row worked, it does become easier. The tension needs to be fairly firm but not too tight, since the beadwork will buckle.

THE BASIC STITCH

Right-angle weave needs practice at first. The basic stitch is a very useful one with a range of applications.

BEADING TIP

If you take the needle through one bead at a time it will encourage a regular shape and pattern, and will help you to see which path to take.

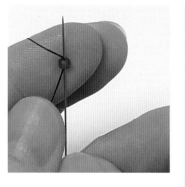

1 Thread a beading needle with 1m (1 yard) of beading thread. Pick up a bead and slide it down to within 15cm (6 inches) of the tail end of the thread. Bring the needle back up through the seed bead creating a loop around the bead. This is now the stop bead.

2 Thread on three more seed beads. Take the needle back through the first (stop bead), second and third beads once more. Pull up into a flat circle.

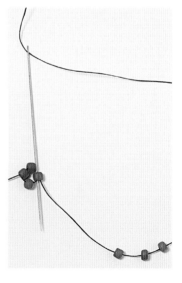

3 Thread on three more seed beads. Take the needle back down through the bead that the working thread is coming out of.

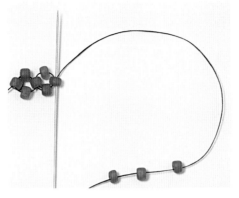

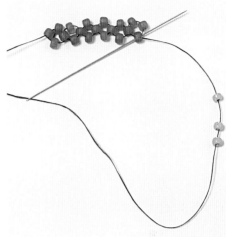

4 Take the needle through the next two beads along. The thread needs to be threaded through at this point to allow you to work the next set of beads along the chain. If you are unsure, just take a moment to work out which bead the thread needs to come out of in order for you to proceed along the row.

5 Add on a further three beads and come back up through the bead the thread is trailing from. Take the needle through the next two beads along and continue in the same manner until you have worked six bead "circles" in total.

6 To start a new row, add the last set of three beads as usual, then pass the needle through the next bead along. Thread on three beads and pass the needle back through the bead the thread is trailing from. Pull up to form a flat circle.

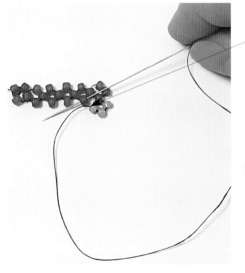

You will notice that there are already two sides of the next circle in place.

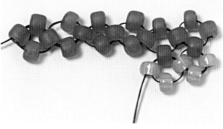

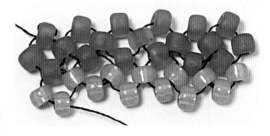

7 Take the needle back through the three beads just added, then through the bottom bead of the next chain of the original row.

8 Thread on two beads now and take the needle back through the two beads already in place, then through the first of the two beads just added.

9 Continue along the row in the same manner. You should start to notice little diamonds forming between the first and second rows. If the thread is crossing these diamonds either vertically or horizontally, the thread path is incorrect. If this is the case you will also notice a stiffening up of the beadwork. The thread must always be worked in alternating circles, never straight up or down.

SQUARE RIGHT-ANGLE WEAVE

This technique is worked in exactly the same way as the basic stitch (page 124–125), only this time using groups of three beads on each side to form squares.

Always thread through three beads at a time to encourage squares to be formed.

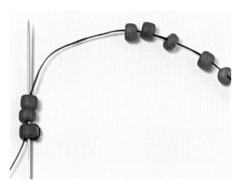

1 Pick up one bead and thread back through it to form the stop bead. Thread on a further 11 beads. Thread through the first set of three beads once more.

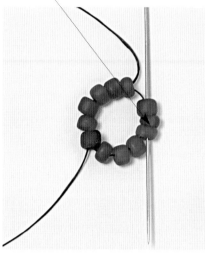

2 Thread through the next six beads, three beads at a time, to keep the square shape of the beadwork.

3 Thread on nine beads – one side of the second square is already in place. Take the needle down through the three beads that form the square wall once again.

4 Thread down through the next two sets of three beads, bringing you into the correct position for the following square. Continue in the same way until the beadwork reaches the desired length.

5 To add the next row, bring the needle just through the three base beads of the square. Thread on nine beads and thread back through the beads the working thread is trailing from.

6 Thread back through all the beads just added, then through the bottom three beads of the next square along on the original row. Continue in the same way to complete the row.

INCREASING ON THE OUTSIDE EDGE

Work right-angle weave as normal. When you reach the end that you want to add an increase, thread through to the side bead of the last set of beads. Thread on three beads, then work back through the bead that the thread is trailing from. When you have added as many increases as you wish, start the next row by attaching the first set of beads to the bottom bead of the last increase.

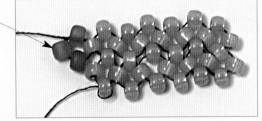

The increase is shown in darker beads.

DECREASING ON THE OUTSIDE EDGE

Work as usual towards the end of the row until you reach the point at which you want to decrease. Simply start the new row from whichever top connecting bead you wish.

INCREASING MID ROW

Work in the usual way, until you reach the point at which you want to increase. Instead of threading two beads for the next circle of beads, thread three beads so that there are two hanging at the bottom of the loop. On return, place a circle of beads through each one of the two bottom beads, thus creating an increase.

Two beads added for increase instead of the usual one bead.

DECREASING MID ROW

This technique is useful for beading over an object. All sorts of shapes can be covered with almost any contours.

The decrease is immediately apparent.

1 Work as usual. When you reach the point at which you require a decrease, thread through two beads – treating them as one – then complete the circle as normal. Pull gently together and continue.

2 Work the next row in the usual way. You can see just how one decrease makes such a difference to the size of the beadwork. This is why this technique is so useful when trying to cover unusual-shaped objects.

TUBULAR RIGHT-ANGLE WEAVE

This stitch is worked using size 11 seed beads, and over an existing
tubular object.

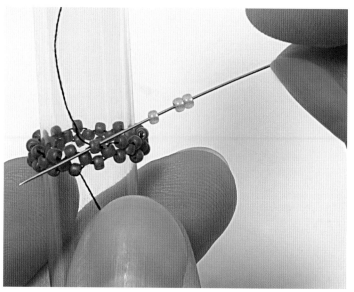

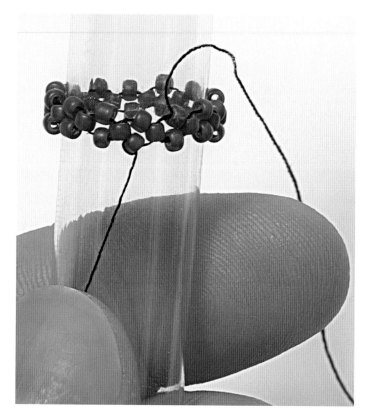

1 First work a flat right-angle weave chain, long enough to fit around the object
you wish to bead. Join together around the tube, taking care to follow the
correct direction of the thread. At this point you could double knot the thread
between two beads for extra stability.

2 With the tail end hanging down towards the base of the object you are about
to bead around, weave the working thread up through one of the beads at the
top of a bead circle. Thread on three seed beads and pass the needle back
through the bead at the top of the original circle, then back through the first
of the three beads just added.

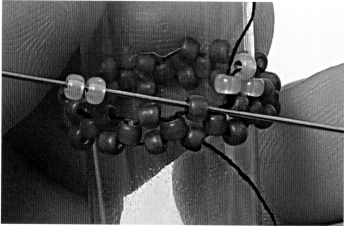

3 Thread on two beads and pass through the next bead along on the
previous row.

4 Pass the needle through the next three beads along on the new row, then through the next bead on the previous row.

The needle is passed diagonally through the two beads to step up to the next row. This happens at the end of every row.

5 Thread on two more beads and bring the needle down through the bead on the side of the last bead circle.

6 Then pass the needle through the next bead on the previous row and up through the first new bead once more, ready to work the next bead circle. Continue in the same way and you will soon see a pattern emerging.

SECTION 3:
Gallery of Finished Works

Designers from around the world have contributed to this selection of inspirational work that demonstrates how the techniques shown in this book can be used to create the most amazing results. You will be able to identify the techniques used to make these pieces and also to understand that all designers have their own special approaches to the use of beads.

BEADED EMBROIDERY

Beaded embroidery is as popular today as it has always been, and the following examples from past and present show just how diverse it can be.

NATALIE (DETAIL) ✧ **LESLEY GEORGE**
The bead embellishment on the motifs of this embroidered section draw the eye towards the centre of the design.

"STARBURSTS" GARMENT
✧ **FROM THE LIBRARY OF KENNETH D. KING**
Dating from the 1940s, this vintage garment is beautifully hand beaded using clear, silver-lined and transparent seed beads, and incorporating silver bugle beads in "starbursts". The bugle beads are true silver-lined beads, but the passage of time has caused them to darken and lose their original beautiful colour.

CREAM CARDIGAN
✧ FROM THE LIBRARY OF KENNETH D. KING

This classic vintage cashmere cardigan dating from the 1950s is lined with silk. The bead embroidery is worked by hand in a baroque-inspired motif. Silver-lined clear and gold seed beads are used together with fringe beads for added movement.

ORGANISM (DETAIL)
✧ LESLEY GEORGE

The mixture of machine embroidery, bead embellishment and textured threads on this hand-dyed fabric creates a beautiful effect.

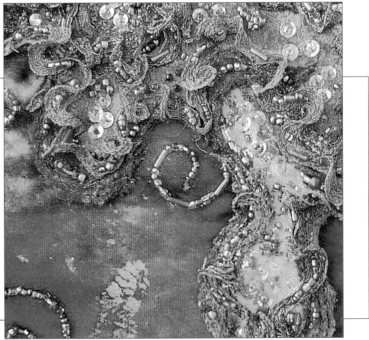

WIRES AND THREADS

A selection of work showing how the techniques from the wiring, knotting and threading sections of the book can be used to create great pieces of jewellery. The potential for diversity quickly becomes apparent when the creativity of the individual artist is added to the mix.

COLOUR CASCADE ✧ JANE OLSON-PHILLIPS

A complex collection of knots has been worked in natural linen thread to highlight the beauty of a Karen Ovington bead and other small beads. You will recognize the half-knots and square knots from the knotting section of this book – others would be covered in a specialist knotting book.

SPIKY NECKLACE ✧ AMANDA GLANVILLE

A freeform wire neckpiece has been created from enamelled wire with contemporary and antique glass beads. The use of simple loops creates a complex and intricate structure.

GRAPEVINE NECKLACE
✧ DIANE FITZGERALD

Art glass leaves and tiny bunches of garnets have been attached to a satin cord that is covered in half-knotting. A strong polyester thread has been used, and the ends of the thread featured as part of the design.

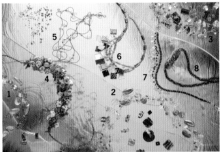

1, 2, 3 MULTISTRAND NECKLACES
✧ MONICA BOXLEY

An assortment of glass beads have been spaced by wrapping fine gauge wire through them twice. The strands of wire have been gathered into a bead at the end to finish them.

4 SUMMER GARDEN ✧ PAULINE HOLT

Several strands of lampworked beads made by the designer have been threaded onto strong thread and half-knotted onto a T-bar fastener to finish.

5 KYNETIC NECKLACE
✧ KATI TORDA

Double strands of beading wire have been crimped at intervals to space blown glass beads.

6 DICHROIC DANGLE NECKLACE
✧ SARA WITHERS

Small pieces of glass have been wired with closed loops to hang from several strands of small beads. These are threaded together through a single strand of beads.

7 COILS AND TRIANGLES NECKLACE
✧ SARA WITHERS

Decorative coils, triangle, and zigzags of wire are finished with closed loops and threaded between simple glass beads.

8 KNITTED WIRE NECKLACE
✧ ELISE MANN

The tube was constructed on a mechanical wire knitter with a feature bead threaded to the centre and other beads pushed down inside the wire, knitted tube.

SILVER DANGLES BRACELET
✧ SARA BENTLEY
A modern take on a charm bracelet. Beads and groups of beads are threaded onto a headpin and attached to the links of a chain with a simple loop.

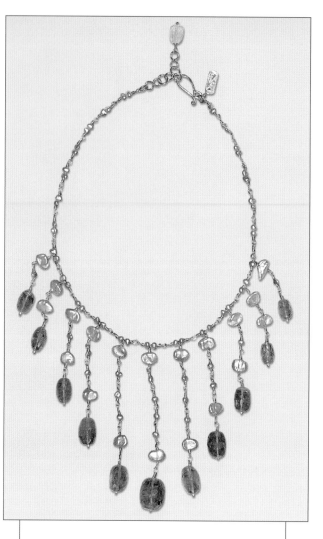

PRINCESS NECKLACE ✧ ANN BIEDERMAN
Closed loops of 22-carat gold wire have been used here to create chains of Keishi pearls that end in faceted emeralds. These hang from a chain of 18-carat wire and pearls.

EASTER EGGS NECKLACE ✧ CYNDI LAVIN
A variation of fringing created this piece which combines vintage lucite and plastic beads. A single strand of beads was threaded onto beading wire, then a new thread was worked up between the beads and more beads were added to this. This thread was then taken back between the main beads. This was repeated throughout the necklace to achieve the unique effect.

AMETHYST NECKLET AND BANGLE ✧ SARA BENTLEY

Different gauges of wire have been twisted and spaced to hold amethyst beads and chips. Several strands of wire and beads are worked together to create the bangle.

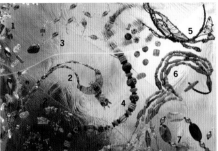

1 AMBER MULTISTRAND NECKLACE ✦ MONICA BOXLEY

Glass and amber beads have been spaced by wrapping fine gauge wire through them twice.

2 PAINTED PIECES ✦ MISHA SEELHOFF

Individual artworks by the maker have been drilled, then strands of small beads used to embroider these pieces until they are worked into one strand to complete the necklace.

3 AMBER TREASURE ✦ MANDY BEACHAM

A jig has been used to form the wire links between the beads and to hold the central polymer bead.

4 MIXED BEAD NECKLACE ✦ SARA WITHERS

A combination of polymer clay, wood, stone and bone beads threaded onto a beading wire.

5 BLACK WAVE TIARA ✦ AMANDA GLANVILLE

This wire headpiece was created from enamelled wire and Swarovski crystal beads.

6 QUEEN OF DJENNE NECKLACE ✦ KATI TORDA

Many strands of clay beads from Mali and brass beads from Ghana have been threaded onto strong thread. The ends were then worked in half-knots.

7 BOHEMIAN RHAPSODY NECKLACE ✦ CYNDI LAVIN

Moakite and Indian glass beads have been finished with wire within a silver tube.

LOOMWORK

The stunning pieces that are shown here have all incorporated the use of a bead loom. The skill and creativity of the designers illustrates the scope of the results that can be achieved.

MIDNIGHT BLUE CHOKER
✦ GILLIAN ASHWELL
A loom-worked choker in iridescent blue bugle and seed beads has been embellished with fringing and fastened with a "button" and loop.

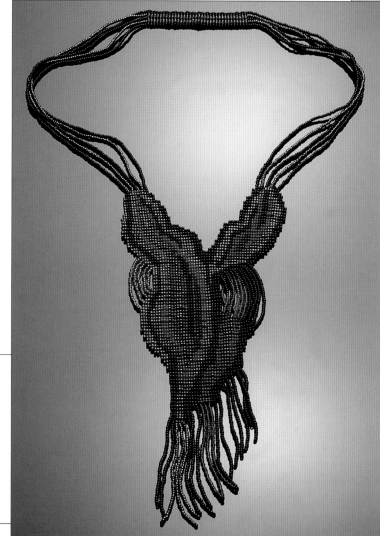

LAVA NECKLACE ✦ SANDRA WALLACE
This asymmetrical necklace has been worked on a loom with size 11 rocailles. The warp threads have also had beads threaded onto them to enhance the design and to create the back of the necklace, with fringing at the front.

THE VALLEY OF THE KINGS
✧ ELEYNE WILLIAMS

A loom-woven wall hanging has been created to juxtapose the painted wood hanger. The bottom of the work has elaborate fringing, and additional warp threads on either side are threaded with clay beads to frame the piece.

ECHOES OF VICTORIA ✧ EVELYN COHEN
Size 11 rocaille and antique glass beads were used to create this loom-woven wall hanging which uses fringing and colour to evoke the Victorian era.

UPON THE MIDNIGHT HOUR ✧ ELEYNE WILLIAMS
This hanging has been created on and off the loom, with additional beaded wefts and fringing. The bugles, beads and mother of pearl pieces have all been combined to fulfill the artist's concept of movement upwards from the forest floor to the planets.

CELTIC BELT ✦ DEBBIE SINISKA

The design for this loomwork will have been worked out on a graph and then repeated. The ends of the belt have been backed with fabric to create the fastener, and the warp threads will have been concealed beneath this backing.

BEADWEAVING PIECES

This section of the Gallery contains a wide variety of pieces created using beadweaving techniques. The artists' work has been chosen to both excite and inspire, illustrating clever use of colour, shape, texture and form, and often combining several techniques that demonstrate just how versatile beadweaving can be.

PALESTINIAN CUSHION ✧ SUE MAGUIRE

The patterns in this piece were taken from traditional Palestinian costumes. Worked in square stitch the cushion really shows the design to its greatest effect, with clean, clear lines. Traditional colours are used and tassels placed at each corner, with a blast of colour at the tips to highlight.

AFRICAN AND VENETIAN MIX NECKLACE ✧ EVELYN COHEN

The main body of this piece is worked in brick stitch, giving strength and support to the fringing that allows the millefiore glass beads to hang freely. The fringe is graduated so that the beads do not knock into each other, a design motif that also shows the full beauty of each individual bead.

PARADISE ISLAND NECKLACE
✧ **STEPHANIE BURNHAM**

*This necklace was created around a beautiful,
hand-blown, glass orchid bead. Two tubular peyote
tubes form the base of the necklace, then the necklace
components were strung together using cording. The
vine was then added, together with the flowers and
loops of seed beads, which represent leaves.*

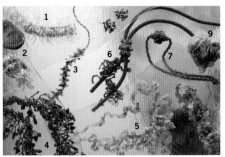

1 FRINGED BRACELET
✧ STEPHANIE BURNHAM
Flat even count peyote forms the base for this cuff bracelet; branch fringing is then added.

2 AGATE SLICES
✧ STEPHANIE BURNHAM
Flat circular peyote with decreasing encases the slices.

3 COLOURED LACE ✧ EVELYN COHEN
Brick stitch triangles are joined together with the artist's own embellishment technique.

4 BOSTON IVY ✧ SANDRA WALLACE
A variation of netting stitch is worked from a central core of beads to create large curls and even spirals.

5 OCEAN WAVES
✧ CHRISTINE BLOXHAM
The beads are made to spiral by using peyote stitch.

6 LARIAT ✧ LYNN FIRTH
Cylinder beads and tubular peyote stitch around a cord form create this piece.

7 CORAL NECKLACE ✧ LYNN FIRTH
The beaded bead of this necklace is constructed using peyote stitch with some decreasing.

8 REFRESHERS ✧ GILLIAN LAMB
Worked in freeform square stitch with the use of several beads of varying sizes, shapes and textures.

9 FLOTSAM AND JETSAM
✧ SANDRA WALLACE
Freeform brick stitch and a peyote ruffle created this vessel.

"BLUE LACE" NECKLACE AND EARRINGS
✧ GILLIAN ASHWELL

*Worked in four colours, with clever use of shading,
this graduated netting piece sits perfectly around the
neckline, with the centre section as the focal point.
The use of the lightest shade in the middle point
draws the eye in.*

YAO NECKLACE ✧ DIANE FITZGERALD

This design is inspired by Yao, an East African tribe.
Techniques used are square stitch and single-needle ladder.
A striking colour combination leads the eye down to the
centre front of the piece, with horizontal stripes and a fringe
bead to finish.

MOORLAND HEATHER HANGING
✧ TESSA HALFPENNEY

This designer takes inspiration from walks on the
Yorkshire moors. Three-drop brick stitch is used to
paint the picture, together with surface embellishment
and heather recreated with branch fringing. The stones
are given a three-dimensional effect with tubular
peyote, squashed and stuffed into shape.

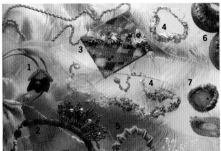

1 TULIP NECKLACE
✧ VARVARA KONSTANTINOV
Tubular peyote stitch with wire forms the base for this necklace. The petals are constructed with peyote stitch – increasing and decreasing shapes the edges.

2 TUBULAR NECKLACE
✧ MISHA SEELHOFF
Tubular peyote stitch is worked over rope to give the tube stability. Fringing added in a random fashion with beads of varying sizes, shapes and textures provides a good contrast to the solidness of the tubing.

3 PATCHWORK BAG ✧ ISOBELLE BUNTING
Peyote stitch with a geometric pattern is echoed in the bag's flap, with the edge softened by the use of branch fringing and accent beads.

4 ABALONE NECKLACE AND BRACELET
✧ CHRISTINE BLOXHAM
Worked in freeform peyote stitch, beads of varying shapes, sizes and textures create a truly organic effect.

5 SPIRAL BRACELET ✧ SUE MAGUIRE
Worked in tubular spiral peyote and peyote stitch, this piece is encouraged to spiral by following the sequence of beads but moving them on one step for each new row.

6 ALI BABA POTS
✧ STEPHANIE BURNHAM
Tubular freeform peyote worked around glass jars, with assorted seed beads giving added texture to the pieces.

7 AGATE SLICES ✧ STEPHANIE BURNHAM
Flat circular peyote is worked directly off the slice, and is then applied to the slice with the use of decreasing.

BEADED RING
✧ FRANÇOISE GOIS

The square design of this ring has been enriched with the use of crystal seed beads.

"GOLDEN TRIO" NECKLACE
✧ VARVARA KONSTANTINOV

Three simple yet stunning leaves form the focal point for this necklace, worked in peyote stitch around the edges with skeleton veins added. The leaves rest on a rope of tubular peyote stitch.

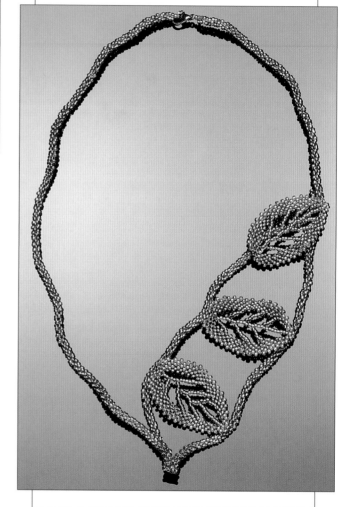

SEAGRASS SET ✧ JUDI WOOD

Freeform right-angle weave worked in layers give great dimension to this piece, along with the addition of precious materials and Japanese seed beads which add texture and colour.

URBAN CHIC NECKLACE ✦ MANDY BEACHAM
This piece is worked entirely in cylinder beads. A beaded bead is stitched in peyote stitch using both increasing and decreasing. The necklace cord is worked in spiral herringbone stitch, with the fastening worked over a wooden bead again in herringbone stitch. At the other end of the necklace the cord breaks into two, and two separate cords are worked until they are the correct length to form a loop to fit over the bead.

RESOURCES

BEADING SOCIETIES

To find out about a group which meets near you, contact your local library. Alternatively, a quick internet search will help with a list of possible societies and groups.

The Bead Society of Great Britain
c/o Carole Morris
1 Casburn Lane
Burwell
Cambs CB5 OED
www.beadsociety.freeserve.co.uk

The Beadworker's Guild
PO Box 24922
London SE23 3WS
Tel: 0870 200 1250
www.beadworkersguild.org.uk

Crafts Council
44A Pentonville Road
London N1 9BY
Tel: 0207 278 7700
www.craftscouncil.org.uk

National Bead Society
3855 Lawrenceville Hwy,
Lawrenceville, GA 30044
Email: ibs@beadshows.com
www.nationalbeadsociety.com

The Bead Society of Greater Washington
The Jennifer Building
400 Seventh Street Northwest
Ground Floor
Washington, DC 20004
Email: info@beadmuseumdc.org

The Los Angeles Bead Society
PO Box 241874
Culver City
CA 90024–9674

The Bead Society of Victoria
PO Box 382
Abbotsford
Victoria 3067
Email: beadsocvic@yahoo.com.au
http://home.vicnet.au/~beadsocv/

SUPPLIERS

The Bead Scene
PO Box 6351
Towcester
Northamptonshire
NN12 7YX
Tel/Fax: 01327 811101
Email: Stephanie@thebeadscene.com
www.thebeadscene.com

Beadworks
16 Redbridge Enterprise Centre
Thompson Close
Ilford, Essex 1G1 1TY
Tel: 0208 553 3240
www.beadworks.co.uk

Beads Unlimited
PO Box 1
Hove
Sussex BN3 3SG
Tel: 01273 740777
www.beadsunlimited.co.uk

Rashbel Marketing
24–28 Hatton Wall
London EC1N 8JH
Tel: 0207 831 5646
www.rashbel.com

Exchange Findings
11–13 Hatton Wall
London EC1N 8HX
Tel: 0207 831 7574

Polymer Clay Pit
3 Harts Lane
Wortham, Diss
Norfolk IP22 1PQ
Tel: 01379 890176
www.polymerclaypit.co.uk

The Bead Shop (retail)
21a Tower Street
Covent Garden
London WC2H 9NS
Tel: 0207 240 0931

Earring Things
Craft Workshops
South Pier Road
Ellesmere Port
Lancashire L65 4FW
www.beadmaster.com

Brighton Bead Shop (retail)
21 Sydney Street
Brighton
Sussex BN1 4EN
Tel: 01273 740777
www.beadsunlimited.co.uk

Kernowcraft

Bolingey

Perranporth

Cornwall

TR6 ODH

www.kernowcraft.com

The Bead Merchant

PO Box 5025

Coggeshall

Essex CO6 1HW

Tel/Fax: 01376 563567

www.beadmerchant.co.uk

The London Bead Co

339 Kentish Town Rd

London NW5 2TJ

Tel: 0870 203 2323

Email: Londonbead@pipex.com

www.londonbeadco.co.uk

GJ Beads

Court Arcade, The Wharf

St Ives

Cornwall TR26 1LG

Tel: 01736 793886

www.gjbeads.co.uk

Pacific Silverworks

461E Main Street Suite A

Ventura, CA 93001

Tel: 805 641 1394

www.pacificsilverworks.com

Beads Galore

2123 S. Priest, Suite 201

Tempe, Arizona 85282

Tel: 480 921 3949

www.beadsgalore.com

Shipwreck Beads

8560 Commerce Place Drive NE

Dept B1 Lacey, WA 98516

Tel: 800 950 4232

www.shipwreckbeads.com

WEBSITES

www.beadwork.about.com

There are plenty of links and articles
on this site.

www.beadingtimes.com

An online beading magazine.

**www.members.cox.net/
sdsantan/beadfairies.html**

A useful resources site with lots of
links and tips.

www.beadexpo.com

An annual conference and bazaar.

INDEX

CREDITS

Authors' Acknowledgments

Sara Withers: Thanks to my co-author, Stephanie Burnham. I am also extremely appreciative of all the work that other designers have sent to us for the Gallery section. I know that it will be truly inspirational and it really is a privilege to be able to show it. It has been good to work with everyone at Quarto again, and to go back to Paul Forrester's photographic studio. Colin Bowling was as patient as ever in producing great photographs from demanding material – especially as he believes that no bead should be smaller than a pea!

Stephanie Burnham: I would like to thank my co-author Sara Withers for all her help and support whilst writing this book; also my family for always believing, and supporting me. Thanks also go to "The Bead Scene" for the beads used in the beadweaving sections of the book.

Quarto would like to thank and acknowledge the following designers for supplying work reproduced in this book:
Kati Torda (1), Mandy Beacham (2, 131), Sandra Wallace (4, 130), and Sue Maguire (160).
Paradise island necklace (147): Glass bead by Carol Fonda and Monty Clarke www.dichroic~glass.com
Beaded ring (154): Original design by Marielle Eloy www.cristaligne.com

In addition to the above, all designers are acknowledged in the captions beside their work.

All photographs are the copyright of Quarto Publishing plc. While every effort has been made to credit contributors, Quarto would like to apologize should there have been any omissions or errors – and would be pleased to make the appropriate correction for future editions of the book.